TALES OF SUB-LIEUTENANT ILYIN

Tales of Sub-Lieutenant Ilyin

by F.F. RASKOLNIKOV

**Translated and annotated
by Brian Pearce**

NEW PARK PUBLICATIONS

Published by New Park Publications Ltd.,
21b Old Town, Clapham, London SW4 0JT

First published in 1934 as
Rasskazy Michmana Il'ina
by 'Sovetskaia Literatura', Moscow

Set up, Printed and Bound
by Trade Union Labour

Distributed in the United States by:
Labor Publications Inc.,
GPO 1876 NY
New York 10001

ISBN 0 86151 025 9

Contents

F.F. Raskolnikov
1892-1939

Fyodor Fyodorovich Ilyin (known to history as 'Raskolnikov') was born in 1892 at Bolshaya Okhta, near St Petersburg. He was the illegitimate son of an Orthodox priest. (Priests of the Orthodox Church have to be married, but are not allowed to re-marry; Raskolnikov's father was a widower.) He was sent to the Prince of Oldenburg's boarding school for deprived children when he was eight years old. His father died when he was fifteen. In 1909 he entered the Economics Department of the St Petersburg Polytechnical Institute. His mother had a hard struggle to keep him and his young brother Alexander, but in consideration of the family's difficulties the board of professors exempted him from tuition fees for several terms.

It was at the Polytechnical Institute (where Struve was one of his teachers) that Raskolnikov read Plekhanov's writings, and went on to discover those of Marx and Engels. At the end of 1910 he joined the RSDLP and began to work on the legal Bolshevik paper *Zvezda* under the guidance of K.S. Yeremeyev, while he was still a student. (V.M. Molotov was one of his comrades in the Bolshevik students' group at the Polytechnical Institute.)

When *Pravda* began, in 1912, Raskolnikov — Ilyin's 'party name' — was one of its original team, working as editorial secretary. After only one month, though, he was arrested and sentenced to three years' exile in Archangel province. His mother managed to get this sentence changed to banishment from Russia, and he set out for Paris. Before he had got far into Germany, however, he was arrested as a Russian spy and sent back. Soon after crossing the border into Russia he fell ill and was taken to a sanatorium. In February 1913 he benefited from the amnesty proclaimed by the Tsar in celebration of the tercentenary of the Romanov dynasty, and so reacquired the right to reside in St Petersburg. He resumed his work for *Pravda*, until it was suppressed at the beginning of the World War.

Called up to the armed forces, he chose the Navy and became a cadet. During his years of training he went on two cruises in Far Eastern waters, visiting Japan and Korea. As described in his book *Kronstadt and Petrograd* (New Park Publications May 1982), the February Revolution found him sitting his final examinations for commissioned rank. His activities during 1917 are related in that book.

In January 1918 it was to Raskolnikov that Lenin assigned the task of reading to the Constituent Assembly the announcement that the Bolshevik fraction was withdrawing therefrom, in the episode recounted in the first of these *Tales*. Soon after this he was made Deputy Commissar for Naval Affairs. We have a record of the impression he made at this time on naval colleagues who did not share his political views. D.N. Fedotov, a former officer of the Imperial Russian Navy, tells us in his autobiography, *Survival Through War and Revolution*, that Captain Behrens, the acting Chief of Naval Staff, said to him that Raskolnikov 'was a decent fellow who did his best and was trying to supplement his lack of knowledge in naval matters by a great deal of reading and discussion with specialists'. Later, Fedotov met Raskolnikov, and says of him: 'I liked Raskolnikov personally: he impressed me as a frank, intellectually honest man.'

During the particularly difficult period when the danger from German imperialism was still strong, Raskolnikov was sent by Lenin on a secret mission to Novorossiisk, to arrange for the scuttling of the Black Sea Fleet, so as to prevent it from falling into the hands of the Germans (see page 16). Speaking about this affair on June 28, 1918, Lenin said to a conference of trade unions and factory committees in Moscow: 'Let me tell you that the man who was operating there was Comrade Raskolnikov, whom the Moscow and Petrograd workers know very well because of the agitation and Party work he has carried on.' In July he was sent to the front against the Czechoslovaks, as a member of the Revolutionary War Council of that front. In August he was appointed commander of the Volga Flotilla, which assisted in the recapture of Kazan in September and chased the enemy flotilla up the River Kama and into the River Byelaya, eventually forcing it to take refuge in Ufa. For these operations Raskolnikov was awarded the Order of the Red Banner, and he was made a member of the Revolutionary War Council of the Republic, with special responsibility for naval affairs.

In December 1918 he set off on a destroyer of the Baltic Fleet, on a reconnaissance mission from Kronstadt to Reval (Tallinn). He was captured by the British naval force operating in those waters and taken to London, where he was at first housed in Brixton Prison. In May 1919, however, after the conditions of British servicemen held in Moscow had been improved, he was allowed to live in a hotel in Gower Street and to receive money from Russia via the Danish Legation. He bought clothes in Oxford Street, and visited the British Museum, the Zoo and Covent Garden, where he heard a performance of *Tosca*. He also visited the headquarters of the British Socialist Party in Drury Lane. Meanwhile Larissa Reisner, who was then Raskolnikov's wife, was agitating strongly for him to be exchanged for the British servicemen in Soviet hands, and after less than a fortnight this was arranged. At the Russo-Finnish border at Byeloostrov he was exchanged for Major Goldsmith, of the British military mission in Caucasia, and some other British servicemen. (See 'A prisoner of the British' in this volume.)

On his return to Russia Raskolnikov was given command of the Volga-Caspian Flotilla, which successfully fought the Whites near Tsaritsyn and Astrakhan, and brought oil from Guriev which was badly needed by Soviet Russia. In May 1920, after the establishment of Soviet power in Baku, he carried out a naval raid on the Iranian port of Enzeli, where some ships of the Whites' Caspian flotilla had taken refuge under the protection of a small British-Indian force. Raskolnikov captured the ships and obliged the British commander, who had been taken completely by surprise, to submit to a capitulation which seriously impaired Britain's prestige in Iran and neighbouring countries. ('The Taking of Enzeli' in this volume.)

Awarded a second Order of the Red Banner for his achievements in the Caspian region, Raskolnikov was now brought back to the Gulf of Finland, as commander of the Baltic Fleet. With the end of the civil war, however, he was transferred to the sphere of diplomacy, his first appointment being Ambassador to Afghanistan. Aided by his wife,

the beautiful and talented Larissa Reisner (who subsequently left him
for Radek), Raskolnikov enjoyed great success in Kabul, and was
decorated by the King. Indeed, he was so successful that one of the
demands of the 'Curzon Note' in 1923 was that he be recalled from
Afghanistan, on the grounds that he was working against British
interests there.

It was largely on the basis of his experiences in Kabul that Raskolnikov wrote the article about the background of the 1928-29 civil
war in Afghanistan which appeared in *Labour Monthly* in 1929 and was
reproduced in *Labour Review* in 1980.

On his return to Moscow, Raskolnikov worked for some years in
the Eastern Department of the Communist International, under the
pseudonym 'Petrov'. He also wrote and did editorial work for the
journals *Molodaya Gvardiya* (*The Young Guard*) and *Krasnaya Nov* (*Red
Virgin Soil*). Then, in 1930, he was returned to the diplomatic sphere,
serving as Soviet representative in Estonia, Denmark and, from 1934,
in Bulgaria.

In July 1937 Raskolnikov was summoned to return to Moscow.
There was considerable delay in his carrying out this order, owing to
the absence of anyone to whom he could hand over his responsibilities
in Sofia, both the First and the Second Secretaries having already
been recalled and not yet replaced. At last, in April 1938, Raskolnikov
set off for Moscow, but before he had crossed the Soviet frontier he
read in the foreign press an announcement that he had been dismissed
from his post: in this announcement he was not given the normal
prefix 'Comrade' . . . He decided not to return until he had managed
to clarify his position, and called first on Litvinov in Geneva and then
on the Soviet Ambassador in Paris, Suritz. He was assured that no
harm would come to him in the USSR, but knowing what had
happened to other Soviet diplomats who had been recalled to Moscow (such as his friends Karakhan and Antonov-Ovseyenko), Raskolnikov still hesitated. Ilya Ehrenburg mentions in his memoirs a
visit from him in Paris, apparently in May 1939. 'I had known some
"deserters" — Besedovsky, Dmitrievsky — but they had been
renegades, men with an uneasy conscience. Raskolnikov was not in
the least like them' — and he adds, characteristically: 'I felt that he

was mentally unbalanced.' A writer in the Paris émigré paper *Voz-rozhdenie* of September 1 1939 reported a conversation he had had with Raskolnikov about this time in which the latter said that Stalin was killing off the old Bolsheviks precisely because of their loyalty to the Party: '*He* is the traitor, not any of his victims.'

On July 17 1939 the Supreme Court of the USSR declared Raskolnikov an outlaw, on the grounds that he had deserted his post, gone over to the camp of the enemies of the people and refused to return to the USSR. He replied by writing a statement of the facts — 'How they made me an "enemy of the people",' dated July 22 — which was published in the Paris émigré paper *Posledniya Novosti*, on July 26. According to *Vozrozhdenie* of September 29 a play by Raskolnikov about Robespierre was being performed 'not long ago' in Paris, but was 'hastily removed from the repertoire' when his outlawry became known.

Towards the end of August it was learnt that Raskolnikov had tried to throw himself out of the window of his hotel room in Grasse, in the South of France, but had been restrained by his wife and hotel staff, and was now in a mental hospital. Interviewed by *Posledniya Novosti* (August 28), another diplomatic 'defector', A.G. Barmin, formerly the Soviet *chargé d'affaires* in Athens, mentioned that he had received a letter from Raskolnikov in late July, asking for advice about how to obtain an international passport. The writer had mentioned that he intended to come to Paris in September and take up literary work. There was nothing in the letter, Barmin said, to suggest mental instability. The interviewer noted that, according to a report, a newspaper had been found in Raskolnikov's hotel room in which passages referring to the German-Soviet Pact were marked. (His 'Open Letter to Stalin' is dated a few days before that event.)

Raskolnikov died in a delirium in a nursing-home in Nice on September 23, 1939. Barmin wrote, in his *One Who Survived*: 'in the opinion of friends, poisoned'.

As Raskolnikov says in his 'Open Letter', he had never belonged to any opposition grouping in the Bolshevik Party. True, in the trade-union discussion of 1920-1921 he had sided with Trotsky, but under Stalin he was, outwardly at least, a loyal Stalinist. Indeed, in 1924 he published in *Krasnaya Nov* a sharply critical review of Trotsky's *Lessons of October* — in which, however, it is apparent that what Raskolnikov most resented was the criticism of Kamenev and Zinoviev, 'Lenin's closest colleagues' and his own friends. In 1927 he criticised Trotsky's politics in a pamphlet on *The Outcome of the Seventh Enlarged Plenum of the Executive Committee of the Communist International*. But his attitude remained free from rancour: Pierre Naville recalls that when, in 1927, he and Gérard Rosenthal, dissident French Communists, spoke at a meeting in Moscow and praised Trotsky, they were approached by Raskolnikov in a spirit of friendly curiosity. All accounts of Raskolnikov by those who knew him agree that his many good qualities never included a head for theory. Until 1937 he does not appear to have been the object of any particular criticism from the Party centre, unless we so categorise the review published in *Krasnaya Letopis* (*Red Annals*) in 1933, of a book of reminiscences Raskolnikov had brought out two years previously. This review, signed by some of his old Kronstadt comrades — P. Smirnov, D. Kondakov, A. Lyubovich, S. Entin and others — complained that he had not properly shown the role played in 1917 by the Party organisation at Kronstadt, but gave readers the impression that everything was done by himself and Semyon Roshal.

During the wave of 'rehabilitations' that followed the Twenty-Second Party Congress (1961), Raskolnikov was one of those who posthumously benefited from the momentarily changed political climate. Books and articles were published about him, and a commission was set up by the Soviet Writers' Union to arrange for publication of Raskolnikov's 'literary heritage'. His widow brought his diary to Russia, and Roy Medvedev quotes a passage from this, about Stalin, in *Let History Judge*. But there was strong resistance in some circles to extending 'rehabilitation' to a man who had, after all, 'defected', one who was, in Soviet language, a 'non-returner'. After the fall of Khrushchev, late in 1964, Raskolnikov again became officially non-existent: he had been, so to speak, de-rehabilitated.

B.P.

Translator's Note

This book is a sequel to *Kronstadt and Petrograd in 1917*. Of the seven items, six are accounts of episodes in the author's own life. The first describes the meeting of the Constituent Assembly, to which Raskolnikov was a deputy, on January 5 (18) 1918. The second deals with the scuttling of the Black Sea Fleet in June 1918, ordered by Lenin so that these ships should not fall into the Kaiser's hands, and organised by Raskolnikov. The subject of the third is an exploit of the Red Flotilla on the river Kama, a tributary of the Volga, in October 1918, when a boatload of Bolshevik prisoners were rescued from captivity in the White Guards' rear. The fourth tale recounts Raskolnikov's capture by the British in the Gulf of Finland in December 1918, his subsequent imprisonment in London in Brixton jail, and his release in exchange for British prisoners. In the fifth item we are taken to the Caspian Sea in May 1920, when a combined operation led by Raskolnikov resulted not only in the recovery of some ships which had been carried off by the Whites to an Iranian port but also in a serious blow to British prestige in the Middle East. These items are in chronological order, but the sixth goes back before the 1917 revolution, to the year 1912, and tells the story of the arrest and imprisonment, in what was then still Petersburg, of the 20-year old Raskolnikov, as a result of his political activities. The book concludes with a piece of fiction, presumably based on an incident the author had read or heard about — an attempt at fraternisation between Russian and Austrian soldiers at Easter 1917.

Published originally in 1934, the book was reissued in 1936, with some changes, and omission of the last two items. Thereafter it was withdrawn from official circulation until 1964, when, during the author's brief 'rehabilitation', an abridged version was published, along with *Kronstadt and Petrograd in 1917*, in a book entitled *At Action Stations*.

Those changes between the editions which seem to be of more than stylistic importance, or made merely for the sake of shortening the text, have been indicated in footnotes.

B.P.

The Tale of a Lost Day*

I

On that bright, frosty January day, people were busily bustling about under the broad glass dome of the Taurida Palace. Moisei Solomonovich Uritsky — short, clean-shaven, with kindly eyes — putting back on his nose his pince-nez, which were attached to his ear by a black cord, and swaying as he walked, passed slowly through the long corridors and well-lit rooms of the palace, and in a hoarse voice gave his final instructions.†

Through the iron gate, beside which a detachment of sailors in black pea-jackets, with machine-gun belts criss-crossed on their chests, were checking tickets of admission, I entered the little square, buried in snow-drifts, in front of the Palace.

Up the low flight of stone steps and past the straight columns of white marble I proceeded into the spacious entrance-hall, took off my overcoat, and, along the ancient winding corridors, which smelt of fresh paint, sought out the commission in charge of the elections to the Constituent Assembly. There they gave me an oblong ticket made of thin green cardboard, bearing Uritsky's signature and the inscription: 'Member of the Constituent Assembly for Petrograd Province'.

---

* ' "Friends, I have lost a day," says an old Latin tag. One cannot help but recall it when one remembers how the fifth of January was lost . . .' (Lenin, 'People from another world,' *Collected Works*, Vol.25, pp.431-433).

† As head of the Petrograd Cheka, Uritsky controlled acess to the Taurida Palace. Only persons who held passes signed by him were allowed into the public galleries.

The huge halls of the palace were filling up with the deputies. The working men and women who had gained entrance with passes issued to the public had already taken their seats in the galleries.

In one of the large rooms the Bolshevik fraction were assembling. Here I met the Central Committee members and the Party's best organisers, Stalin and Sverdlov.* The delegates from Moscow — Skvortsov-Stepanov, Bubnov, Lomov, Varvara Yakovleva — kept close together.

Lenin, wearing a padded overcoat with a lambskin collar and a big fur hat with earflaps, entered at a brisk pace and, after nodding to comrades and shaking their hands quickly, then modestly went to his seat, took off his coat, and carefully laid it over the back of the chair.

The winter sunshine and the soft heaps of snow, lying outside the windows, which it caused to sparkle blindingly, made the room unusually bright.

Yakov Mikhailovich Sverdlov, in a glossy black leather jacket, placed his warm fur hat on the table and declared the fraction-meeting open.

Discussion of the agenda began. Someone set forth a plan for how we should work if the Constituent Assembly were to enjoy a protracted existence. Bukharin stirred impatiently on his chair and lifted his finger to ask permission to speak. 'Comrades,' he said, in an angry and sarcastic tone, 'do you really think we are going to waste an entire week here? We'll be here for three days at the most.' A quizzical smile played on Vladimir Ilyich's pale lips. Comrade Sverdlov, holding in both hands a typewritten sheet of paper, slowly read out the declaration of the rights of the working people.† His full lips, bordered with black moustaches and a pointed black beard,

---

* The 1964 edition omits the phrase 'the Party's best organisers'.

† The text of the 'Declaration of the Rights of the Working and Exploited People', which had been adopted on January 3 (16) 1918 by the Central Executive Committee of the Congress of Soviets, is given in Lenin's *Collected Works* (4th edition, English version), Vol.25, pp.423-425.

Lenin with Sverdlo
in 19

Y.M. Sverdlov

moved expressively. This declaration of rights, which was to be presented to the Constituent Assembly, consolidated all the acts taken by the Soviet power in relation to peace, land and workers' control in the enterprises. When he had finished reading it, Sverdlov slowly sat down and, taking his pince-nez from his nose and wiping them with his handkerchief, looked benevolently about the room with his lively but rather tired dark eyes.

After a brief debate, the Bolshevik fraction voted that, if the Constituent Assembly should fail to accept the declaration that day, we must immediately walk out of it.

We adopted without debate a decision not to put forward a candidate of our own for the chairmanship of the Constituent Assembly, but to support Maria Spiridonova, the candidate of the Left SR fraction.

Somebody reported that all the leaders of the Right SRs had arrived in the palace: Viktor Chernov, Bunakov-Fundaminsky and Gotz. We were amazed at the impudence shown by Gotz, who had led the revolt of the military cadets and then gone underground for some time, but now unexpectedly surfaced.

Suddenly we learnt that the SRs had organised a demonstration which was advancing on the Taurida Palace with anti-Soviet slogans. Soon afterwards the news was brought that this demonstration had been dispersed, at the corner of Kirochnaya Street and Liteiny Avenue, by Red troops who fired in the air.* On the bronze dial of the clock the hand was approaching four.

We were summoned to proceed without delay into the hall, as the deputies had already assembled and were getting restless, and even wanted to open the proceedings on their own. We broke off our meeting and entered the hall.

---

* According to other Bolshevik sources, seven or eight persons were killed when this demonstration was dispersed. The dead included G.I. Logvinov, a Socialist-Revolutionary peasants' leader, and a girl student, also an SR activist, named Gorbachevskaya. Non-Bolshevik accounts claim that nearly one hundred people were killed or wounded.

II

The immense amphitheatre, with its glass ceiling and stout white columns, was full of people. There were empty seats only on the left wing. Our sector took up a third of the hall. The SRs were seated in the centre and on the right. In the front row, with his head held high and smiling broadly, Viktor Chernov was talking with friends. Bunakov-Fundaminsky, his long hair combed back, was examining something closely through his pince-nez. The round, rather swarthy face of Gotz expressed inner excitement and alarm, in spite of his attempt to appear composed. The crowded galleries were motley with blouses of black cloth and Russian shirts of coloured sateen.

Amid conversation and joking and the banging of desk-lids, we slowly made our way to our seats. Suddenly, in the middle of the hall, where the SRs were, arose a narrow-shouldered person who, in a voice full of rancour and irritation, impatiently announced: 'Comrades, it's now four o'clock. We propose that the oldest member open this session of the Constituent Assembly.'

The SRs were evidently prepared for a triumph, and had distributed the roles among themselves. As though at a signal, a decrepit old man, all overgrown with hair and with a long grey beard, clambered awkwardly and short of breath on to the high tribune. It was the Zemstvo worker and former member of Narodnaya Volya, Shvetsov. Comrade Sverdlov, who was supposed to open the proceedings, had lingered somewhere and was late.

With an old man's trembling hand Shvetsov picked up the chairman's bell and shook it hesitantly: its clear tinkling sound rang through the hall.

The SRs intended to open the Constituent Assembly independently of the Soviet power. To us, on the contrary, it was important to emphasise that the Constituent Assembly was being opened not on its own initiative but by the will of the All-Union Central Executive Committee of the Soviets, which had no intention of handing over to this Assembly its rights as master of the Soviet land.

When we saw that Shvetsov was seriously going to open the proceedings, we started frenzied interruptions. We shouted, whistled, stamped our feet and banged our fists on the thin wooden lids of the desks. When all that failed to do the trick, we leapt to our feet and rushed towards the tribune with shouts of 'Get down!' The Right SRs hurled themselves forward to defend their *doyen*. A certain exchange of fisticuffs took place on the parapet-covered steps of the tribune.

Shvetsov rang his bell in dismay and soundlessly, helplessly moved his pale, quivering lips. We drowned with our uproar his feeble old man's voice. One of us grabbed Shvetsov by the sleeve of his jacket and tried to drag him from the tribune. Then, suddenly, beside the portly, podgy Shvetsov, there appeared, up there on the tribune, the lean, narrow-shouldered figure of Sverdlov, in his black leather jacket. In a masterfully confident manner he took the bright nickel-plated bell from the dumbfounded old man and with a careful but firm gesture moved Shvetsov out of his way.

A furious din, with shouts, protests and banging of fists on desks, arose from the benches of the indignant SRs and Mensheviks. But Sverdlov stood firm on the tribune, like a marble monument, calm and unmoved, looking around at his adversaries, with an expression of provocative mockery, through the large, oval lenses of his pince-nez. Coolly he rang the bell, and with a sweeping, authoritative gesture of his thin, hairy hand he silently called the Assembly to order. When the noise gradually subsided, Sverdlov addressed the entire hall, with unusual dignity, in his loud, distinct bass voice. 'The Executive Committee of the Soviets of Workers' and Peasants' Deputies has authorised me to open the proceedings of the Constituent Assembly.'

'There's blood on your hands! There's been enough bloodshed!' the Mensheviks and SRs squealed hysterically, like dogs whose tails had been trodden on. Loud applause from our benches drowned these hysterical lamentations.

'The Central Executive Committee of the Soviets of Workers' and Peasants' Deputies . . .', Comrade Sverdlov rapped out solemnly in his metallic voice.

'A fraud,' yelped some SR in a thin, piercing falsetto.

'. . . expresses the hope,' Comrade Sverdlov went on, undisturbed, in the same firm tone as before, 'that the Constituent Assembly will fully recognise all the decrees and decisions of the Council of People's Commissars. The October Revolution has kindled the fire of socialist revolution not only in Russia but in all countries.'

On the right-wing benches someone sniggered. Yakov Mikhailovich, fixing him with a crushing, contemptuous glance, raised his voice:

'We do not doubt that sparks from our conflagration will fly all over the world, and that the day is not far distant when the working classes of all countries will rise up against their exploiters just as in October the Russian working class rose up, followed by the Russian peasantry.'

Triumphant applause broke from us like a migrant flock of white swans suddenly taking off into the sky.

'We do not doubt,' went on the chairman of the Central Executive Committee, still more boldly and confidently, as though catching fire from the gunpowder of his own words, 'that the true representatives of the working people who are sitting here in the Constituent Assembly are bound to help the Soviets to put an end to class privileges. The representatives of the workers and peasants have acknowledged the right of the working people to the means and instruments of production, ownership of which has hitherto enabled the ruling classes to exploit the working people in every way. Just as, in their day, the French bourgeoisie, at the time of the great revolution of 1789, proclaimed a declaration of rights for freedom to exploit the people, who were deprived of the instruments and means of production, so our Russian Socialist revolution must make its own declaration.'

Again, all the members of our fraction applauded warmly.

The other fractions, suspicious, maintained a hostile silence.

'The Central Executive Committee expresses the hope that the Constituent Assembly, in so far as it correctly expresses the interests of the people, will associate itself with the declaration which I am now to have the honour to read to you,' said Comrade Sverdlov. Calmly and solemnly, without haste, he then read the declaration, ending his address with these words: 'By authority of the All-Russia Central Executive Committee of the Soviet of Workers', Soldiers' and Peasants' Deputies, I declare the Constituent Assembly open.'

We rose to our feet and sang the *International*. All the members of the Constituent Assembly also got up, with a loud cracking sound as their folding seats sprang back, and one after another they discordantly took up the anthem. Slowly and triumphantly the solemn sounds of the hymn of the international proletariat floated into the air.

In the centre of the hall, in the front row, standing with his stout legs apart and tossing high his curly, greying head, complacently singing and archly smiling, his mouth wide open, was the leader of the Right SRs, Viktor Chernov, that 'Likhach Kudryavich'.* Carried away by the pleasure of the occasion, he closed his eyes like a nightingale absorbed in its singing. Sometimes he turned his obese body towards the other deputies and conducted their singing with his thick, stumpy fingers, like a psalm-reader functioning as precentor with the choir of a parish church.

> *'No yésli gróm velíkiy gryánet*
> *'Nad sbóroy psóv i palachéy,'†*

sang the Constituent Assembly.

---

* It is not clear what the author means by this epithet. Possibly 'Curly the Daredevil', or else 'Kudeyar's daredevil son' — Kudeyar being a famous brigand in Russian folklore.

† From the Russian version of the *International*. Literally, it means: 'But if the mighty thunder crashes over the pack of curs and hangmen'; the verse goes on to say that 'the sun will still warm us with its rays'. Compare this verse from the American version of the song: 'How many on our flesh have fattened!/But if the bloody birds of prey/Shall vanish from the sky one morning,/The golden sun will stay.'

At these words Viktor Chernov slyly screwed up his cunning, knavish little eyes, flashed them with his usual provocative skittishness and, finally, with a challenging smile on his full, voluptuous lips, demonstratively made a sweeping gesture in our direction.

When the singing ended we cried out loudly: 'Long live the Soviets of Workers', Peasants' and Soldiers' Deputies: All power to the Soviets!'

'All power to the Constituent Assembly!' the Right SR Bykhovsky angrily shouted from his seat.

Sverdlov restored silence by loudly saying: 'Allow me to express the hope that the foundations of the new society outlined in this declaration, will remain unshakeable and, having become established in Russia, will gradually establish themselves throughout the world.'

'Long live the Soviet Republic!' Once more the slogan rose from our benches in a unanimous, triumphant shout. And, in our enthusiasm, we clapped our hands unsparingly, with deafening effect.

II

The Right SR Lordkipanidze raised a point of order.* When he reached the tribune he spoke hastily and excitedly, as though afraid that he was about to be deprived of the right to speak. Angrily he said: 'The SR fraction would have thought that the Constituent Assembly should have begun its work long before this. We consider that the Constituent Assembly can itself open its own proceedings: there is no other authority but that of the Constituent Assembly empowered to open them.'

The indignation that filled us burst forth. Whistling, uproar, shouts of 'Get down!', rattling and banging of desks drowned the speaker's words. Behind him, on the high-placed chairman's seat, Sverdlov remained unmoved. To observe the

---

* This was S.M. Lordkipanidze — not to be confused with two other politicians with this surname who were active in the same period.

proprieties he rang his nickel-plated bell and, turning towards us his cheerful, merrily smiling eyes, offhandedly let fall, with assumed impartiality: 'I must ask you to be quiet.'

In the silence that followed, Lordkipanidze, without turning round, pointed over his shoulder with the thumb of his right hand at Sverdlov, and scornfully remarked: 'In view of the fact that the citizen who is behind me is directing . . .'

This insolence caused us finally to lose all control of ourselves. Lordkipanidze's concluding words were drowned in a fearful, inhuman roar and din, in a frenzied racket and loud, piercing whistles.

With amazing restraint, Yakov Mikhailovich ignored the challenging allusion to himself and, in the calm tones of a man confident of his powers, said: 'I humbly request you to be quiet. If necessary I will myself, using the power conferred on me by the Soviets, call the speaker to order. Be so good as not to make noises.'

The uproar ceased, and Lordkipanidze, in a choking voice, expressed his anger at the reading of the declaration: 'We consider,' he concluded, 'that the election of the chairman should proceed under the preliminary chairmanship of the oldest deputy. However, gentlemen, we shall not give battle on that question, as you may have wished us to do, we won't let ourselves be caught by that trick, thereby providing you with a formal excuse to break with the Constituent Assembly.'

Lordkipanidze left the tribune. On his thin, sharp face shone the consciousness of duty performed. In the centre and on the right of the Assembly he was received back with applause. Lordkipanidze's speech showed me what the Right SRs game was. It became clear that they had decided to 'maintain in being' the Constituent Assembly, just as in their time the Cadets had kept the First Duma* going. They wanted to use

* 'First' is probably a slip of the pen for 'Second'. When the Second State Duma met, in February 1907, the Cadets adopted a policy of 'making it last as long as possible' by avoiding too flagrant provocation of the Tsar's government — in spite of which the assembly was dissolved in June.

the Constituent Assembly as their legal basis for overthrowing Soviet power. And I recalled how, a few days before the opening of the Constituent Assembly, I had had to argue till I was hoarse with some SRs in the red-brick barracks of the 2nd Baltic Depot, beside the remote and deserted Crooked Canal. The Right SRs were then going all out, waging a desperate, adventuristic struggle to win over the Petrograd garrison. The underground military organisation of the SRs was striving to get a foothold in every army unit. A meeting of the sailors of the 2nd Baltic Depot was attended by all the great men of the Right SRs, headed by Brushvit, a member of the Constituent Assembly. They were expecting Viktor Chernov, but for some reason he did not turn up. In a cheerless corridor, dimly lit by electric lamps, I unexpectedly encountered the young SR Lazar Alyansky, who, his hands in the pockets of his flared trousers, was strolling about with an important air, dressed in the dark-blue jumper of a sailor, his collar turned outside. When he met me he looked embarrassed, and blushed.

'Why are you wearing naval uniform?' I asked him, in amazement.

Alyansky grew even more confused. 'I've just joined the Navy,' he said, looking me boldly in the eyes and, as always, speaking with a strong burr.

I could not repress a smile.

In order to get into the barracks the SRs were at that time making extensive use of their very own version of 'going to the people',* which became in practice nothing but a masquerade.

The meeting opened soon after this. From the low platform of the sailors' club the SRs poured forth their burning speeches, with the merciless howling of provincial tragedians and the loud wailing of hysterical churchwomen, and with frenzied beating of their well-fleshed breasts.

'You Bolsheviks have blood on your hands,' growled one

---

* In 1873 the SRs' spiritual fathers, the Narodniks, organised what they called a 'going to the people', when several thousand young people from the intelligentsia went into the villages to mix with peasants and try to spread revolutionary ideas among them.

Right SR orator, shaking his finger. But these reproaches and accusations met with no sympathy among the sailors. Even the young sailors who had been called up in the autumn were firmly for Soviet power and for the Bolshevik Party. Nor did Alyansky's self-sacrificing masquerade prove to be of any help. The SRs suffered a striking defeat in the 2nd Baltic Depot. Even the Preobrazhensky and Semyonovsky Regiments, on which the Right SR leaders relied most of all, disappointed them. Despite the tireless, frenzied activity of the SRs, on the day that the Constituent Assembly met not a single unit of the Petrograd garrison, for all their waverings, agreed to give support to the party of Kerensky and Chernov.

IV

Ivan Ivanovich Skvortsov-Stepanov slowly mounted the tribune. Turning his whole body towards the right-wing benches and nervously jerking his close-cropped grey head, he spoke with great feeling, rising to passion, to expose the hypocrisy of the Right SRs.*

'Comrades and citizens!' boomed Skvortsov-Stepanov, loudly and clearly, emphasising his words with vigorous gestures of his long, thin hand. 'I must first express my astonishment that the citizen who spoke before me threatened to break with us if we took certain steps. Citizens sitting on the right! The break between us has been consummated long since. You were on one side of the barricades, with the White Guards and the military cadets, and we were on the other, with the soldiers, workers and peasants.'

In passing, Ivan Ivanovich, being a theoretician, gave his opponents a lesson in elementary politics: 'How can you,' he wondered, 'appeal to such a concept as the will of the whole people? For a Marxist "the people" is an inconceivable notion: the people does not act as a single unit. The people as a unit is a

---

* According to Krupskaya's *Reminiscences of Lenin*, Skvortsov-Stepanov did not speak until after the election of Chernov as chairman, and he was preceded by Bukharin and the Menshevik Tsereteli.

mere fiction, and this fiction is needed by the ruling classes. It is all over between us,' he summed up. 'You belong to one world, with the cadets and the bourgeoisie, and we to the other, with the peasants and the workers.'

He articulated those last words with special distinctness, abruptly and sharply. His entire speech, delivered with tremendous *élan*, made a very powerful impression. Afterwards Skvortsov-Stepanov told me, with pride, that his speech had been approved by Lenin.

Comrade Sverdlov, putting aside the sandglass, proposed that we proceed to the election of a chairman. Each fraction appointed two representatives to act as tellers. Our fraction chose me and P.G. Smidovich. He had soft grey hair and blue, short-sighted eyes which always looked surprised, behind the round lenses of his gold-rimmed spectacles. We ascended the steps of the tribune, where two wooden boxes were placed and hidden on one side by a curtain of black calico. These were the ballot-boxes. One bore the inscription 'Chernov', the other 'Spiridonova'. In the stern tones of a teacher Sverdlov called the deputies up in alphabetical order. At the tribune they received from us two balls, one black and one white. Each deputy dropped his white ball, in favour of election, into one box, and his black ball, against election, into the other.

Sverdlov, who was obviously bored with this wearisome procedure, summoned the deputies faster and faster, so that soon there was a long queue in front of the ballot-boxes. At last the voting was completed. With a sigh of relief we set about counting the balls in the two boxes. Then we informed Sverdlov of the result.

With his chairman's bell he invited all to resume their seats and in his metallic voice impassively said: 'Permit me to announce the results of the voting. For Chernov there were 244 votes in favour of his election and 151 against. For Spiridonova there were 151 votes in favour of her election and 244 against. Consequently, Constituent Assembly member Chernov has been elected. I invite him to take his place.'

And Yakov Mikhailovich stepped down with dignity from the chairman's seat, giving way to a beaming Chernov. Without sitting down Chernov delivered a flowery speech. He was evidently not in good form that day, and spoke flabbily, with difficulty and strain, working himself up artificially in the most emotional passages. 'All the weary, those who must return to their homes, those who cannot live without that, just as the hungry cannot live without food . . .' he orated.

'He can't call a spade a spade,' I thought, weary of this monotonous and dreary rhetoric. And I recalled that long-haired phrasemonger Professor Valentin Speransky, the idol of the first-year Bestuzhev girls,* who, even at home, would say, when ill, in his bombastic 'lofty style': 'I have been overtaken by a malignant influenza.'

'The very fact that the first session of the Constituent Assembly has opened proclaims the end of civil war among the peoples who inhabit Russia,' declaimed Viktor Chernov mellifluously as he cast his wide-open eyes in triumph around the hall. The audience was not particularly attentive: even the SRs chattered among themselves, yawned, or left the hall. Our people continually interrupted him with scornful laughter, ironical remarks and mockery.

The public who filled the galleries were also bored by Chernov's empty and tedious verbiage, and kept answering him back from up there. He lost patience, invited the interrupters to go away, and at last threatened 'to raise the question whether some persons here are in a condition to conduct themselves as befits members of the Constituent Assembly'.

Chernov's impotent threats eventually caused us to lose control of ourselves, and the resulting uproar smothered his voice. Like a drowning man clutching at a lifebelt he snatched up the chairman's bell and tinkled it — then helplessly sank back into the broad and massive armchair, so that only his shaggy grey head was visible. :

---

* The 'Bestuzhev higher-education courses for women', established in Petersburg in 1879, were so named after their first director, K.N. Bestuzhev-Ryumin.

V

A succession of dull speeches dripped upon us in the hall, like doleful autumn rain. Long since had the electric lights been lit: they were concealed behind the cornices of the glass ceiling, and illuminated the hall with a suffused radiance. Increasingly the soft, restful seats in the great amphitheatre were being deserted. Members went for a stroll across the smooth, slippery, brilliantly clean parquet of the luxurious Catherine Hall, with its round marble columns; they were drinking tea and smoking in the buffet, and unburdening their hearts in conversation with their party colleagues.

We were summoned to a meeting of our fraction. On Lenin's initiative we resolved to quit the Constituent Assembly on the grounds that it had rejected the declaration of the rights of the working and exploited people. Lomov and I were entrusted with the task of announcing our departure. Somebody proposed that we all return to the meeting-hall, but Vladimir Ilyich stopped us from doing that.

'Don't you realise,' he said, 'that if we go back in there, and then, after reading our statement, walk out of the hall, the sailors on guard, electrified by our action, will at once, on the spot, shoot down everybody who stays behind? We must not do that, on any account,' said Vladimir Ilyich in a categorical tone. After the fraction meeting I and other members of the government were called to the Ministerial wing of the palace for a meeting of the Council of People's Commissars. I was at that time Deputy People's Commissar for Naval Affairs. (*Zamkom po morde*** was how certain wits abbreviated my title).

The meeting of the Council of People's Commissars began with Lenin, as always, in the chair. He sat by the window, at a desk which was lit with a soft, homely light, by a table lamp with a round green shade.

---

* Acronyms of the titles of institutions and appointments enjoyed a great vogue in Russia at this time. The acronym of Raskolnikov's title produces words meaning 'with a lock on his snout'.

There was only one item on the agenda: what was to be done with the Constituent Assembly after our fraction's departure from it?

Vladimir Ilyich proposed that the Assembly be not dispersed but allowed to spend that night in talk for as long as they liked. Then the members should be allowed freely to go home. But when morning came, nobody should be allowed back into the Taurida Palace. The Council of People's Commissars adopted Lenin's proposal. It was time for Lomov and me to go into the meeting hall. 'Right, then — off you go,' were Vladimir Ilyich's parting words.

Armed with the typewritten text of our statement, we two hastened into the meeting hall, while all the other Bolsheviks made their way into the corridors. I agreed with Lomov that I should be the one to read out our statement.

On entering the hall we went to the Government box, which was situated next to the tribune. With a badly sharpened pencil I scribbled on a piece of paper torn from my notebook: 'On the instructions of the Bolshevik fraction I ask permission to make a special statement. Raskolnikov.'

Rising on tiptoe I reached out to hand this message to a grave, already no longer smiling Chernov, who sat up there on the high platform, looking as majestically severe as an Egyptian priest during the performance of some solemn rite. When the member who was speaking had finished, Chernov announced: 'I call on Constituent Assembly member Raskolnikov to make a special statement.'

I mounted the tribune and, in a quite ordinary voice, without false emotionalism, but as clearly and expressively as I could, I read the statement about our departure from the Assembly, stressing the most important passages.* Conscious of the seriousness of the document they were hearing read to them, everyone in the hall pricked up their ears and at once stopped talking.

---

* The text of the declaration read by Raskolnikov is given in Lenin's *Collected Works*, Vol.25, pp.429-430.

The empty benches on the left side of the hall, where the Bolsheviks had been sitting not long before, yawned like a black abyss. In his sailor's cap, worn at a jaunty angle and with a thick tuft of jet-black hair sticking rakishly out from under it, and with his chest swathed in machine-gun belts, the cheerful commander of the guard, Zheleznyakov, stood by the door. Beside him were clustered in the doorway several Bolshevik deputies, tensely observing what was happening in the hall.

Amid deathly quiet I openly called the SRs enemies of the people, who had refused to accept as binding upon them the will of the immense majority of the working people. The entire hall was frozen into silence.

Despite the sharp language of our statement, nobody interrupted me. After explaining that we were not taking the path of the Constituent Assembly, which reflected the yesterday of the revolution, I announced our departure, and got down from the tribune. The public in the galleries, which had met every sentence of my statement with loud applause, now raved with joy, quickly and deafeningly clapping their hands, stamping their feet and shouting 'Bravo!' and 'Hurrah!'.

One of the sailors in the guard raised his rifle to his shoulder and took aim at bald-headed Minor, who was sitting on the right-wing benches. Another sailor angrily grabbed the rifle, saying: 'Put it down, you fool!'

VI

In the Ministerial wing Vladimir Ilyich, wearing a black overcoat with an Astrakhan collar and a hat with earflaps, gave us our last instructions.

'I am leaving now, but you must keep an eye on your sailors,' said Comrade Lenin to me, with a smile. 'There is no need to disperse the Constituent Assembly: just let them go on chattering as long as they like and then break up, and tomorrow we won't let a single one of them come in.'

Vladimir Ilyich gave me a firm handshake and then, leaning

Uritsky *Dybenko*

against the wall, put on his galoshes and went out through the snow-laden porch of the Ministerial wing into the street.

A frosty freshness burst in through the half-open door, which was covered with felt and oilcloth. Then, with a slight squeak of its spring, the heavy door closed. The dimly-lit entrance-hall was left filled with piercing cold and the sharp smell of frost.

Moisei Solomonovich Uritsky, screwing up his short-sighted eyes and adjusting his dangling pince-nez, took me gently by the arm and invited me to have tea with him. Through a long corridor with glass walls, like an orangery, we made our way round the meeting-hall, which was still rustling with long-winded speeches, crossed in a leisurely way the broad Catherine Hall with its white marble columns, and sat ourselves down in a spacious side-room. Uritsky poured me some tea and, with his mild, shy smile, offered me a plate of thinly-sliced pieces of lemon. Stirring our glasses with our spoons, we got down to a heart-to-heart talk.

Suddenly into our room came, with quick, firm tread, Dybenko — a strapping, broad-shouldered figure with thick black hair and a short, neatly-clipped beard, and wearing a new, grey winter overcoat gathered at the waist.

Choking with laughter he told us, in his booming bass voice, that the sailor Zheleznyakov had just gone up to the chairman of the Assembly, placed his broad hand on the shoulder of a Chernov numb with astonishment, and said to him in a peremptory tone: 'The guard are tired. I propose that you close the meeting and let everybody go home.'

Viktor Chernov

With trembling hands Chernov hastily gathered up his papers and declared the meeting closed. It was 4.40a.m. A starry, frosty night looked in through the curtainless windows of the palace. The happy deputies rushed noisily to the cloak-room, where sleepy porters in shabby gilded liveries slackly helped them on with their overcoats.

In England there was once a 'Long Parliament'. The Constituent Assembly of the RSFSR was the shortest parliament in the entire history of the world. It ended its inglorious and joyless life after 12 hours and 40 minutes.

When, in the morning, Dybenko and I told Vladimir Ilyich of the miserable way the Constituent Assembly had ended, he screwed up his dark eyes and at once grew cheerful.

'Did Viktor Chernov really submit unquestioningly to the guard-commander's demand, without making the slightest attempt to resist?', Lenin asked, in amazement. And, leaning right back in his chair, he laughed long and infectiously.*

---

* An account of the meeting of the Constituent Assembly as seen from the SRs' point of view is given by O.H. Radkey in *The Sickle under the Hammer* (1963), Chapter VIII.

The Fate of the Black Sea Fleet

I

One day at the beginning of June 1918 Comrade Lenin telephoned me and told me to come and see him at once. I went out
into the street. It was a warm, sunny day. The shadows of the
trees lay like lace on the worn flagstones of the pavement.
Passing under the vaulted archway of the white Kustafya
Tower,* I showed my cardboard permanent pass to the Red
Army soldier, armed with a rifle, who stood on guard, and then,
through the Troitsky Gate, on which at that time still hung a
large icon, darkened by time, made my way up the steep
approach to the Kremlin.

The broad courtyard, paved with large cobblestones, was
deserted. Ancient guns with long barrels extending horizon-
tally were lined up, like soldiers, in front of the high barrack
buildings. The wide muzzle of the Tsar-Cannon† showed black
on its short carriage, before which rose a pyramid of heavy,
round iron cannon balls. I entered by the corner door of the
Council of People's Commissars, went up the stairs and, along
a corridor carpeted with new matting, made my way to the
spacious reception-room, furnished with tables and cupboards,
of Vladimir Ilyich's office. Comrade Glyasser went in to report
my arrival. A minute later she emerged from Lenin's work-
room and, adjusting her pince-nez, said: 'Vladimir Ilyich asks
you to go in.'

I opened the door through which Comrade Glyasser had
returned and, across a carpet which muffled my footsteps,

---

* The Kustafya Tower is the barbican of the Troitsky Gate of the Kremlin.
† The Tsar-Cannon, cast in 1586, is one of the largest cannon ever made, and along
with the Tsar-Bell, the largest bell in the world, is one of the 'sights' of the Kremlin.

traversed a conference-room in the midst of which stood a long table covered with thick green cloth. When I reached the opposite end of the room I knocked softly and cautiously on the white, two-leaved door.

'Come in,' said Vladimir Ilyich in his deep, pleasant voice. I opened the door and went into the brightly-lit work-room. Vladimir Ilyich was sitting at a desk, on a wooden chair with a round back. In front of him stood, symmetrically placed, two low leather armchairs for visitors. At the side was a small revolving bookcase filled with books. The brand-new book-cases ranged along the wall contained more books, tidily arranged. On the wall beside the entrance-door a map of Russia showed green.

When I appeared, Vladimir Ilyich looked up, gently squeezed my hand and asked me to sit down. I settled into one of the low leather armchairs.

'I sent for you because things are going badly at Novoros-siisk,' said Vladimir Ilyich, anxiously stroking his head and fixing me with his deep, dark eyes. 'Vakhrameyev* and Glebov-Avilov have wired that the plan to scuttle the Black Sea Fleet is meeting with a lot of resistance from a section of the crews and from all the White-Guard-minded officers. There is a strong tendency in favour of going to Sebastopol. But taking the fleet to Sebastopol means handing it over to German imperialism. We can't allow that to happen. It is necessary, at all costs, to scuttle the fleet: otherwise, it will fall into the hands of the Germans. Here is a coded message we have just received from Berlin . . . Joffe wires that the German Government is categorically demanding that the Black Sea fleet be transferred from Novorossiisk to Sebastopol.'

Vladimir Ilyich briskly extracted the deciphered copy of Joffe's telegram from a heap of papers and, holding it in both hands, read it out to me.

The German Government was peremptorily insisting that, not later than June 18, the entire Black Sea fleet be transferred

---

* Vakhrameyev, I.I., 1885-1965. He reached Novorossiisk on June 2.

to Sebastopol, which was held by the Germans and where it would be interned until the end of the war. If the fleet remained in Soviet-held Novorossiisk after that day, the German imperialists threatened to seize the ships by armed force.

'You must leave today for Novorossiisk,' said Lenin, in a decisive tone that brooked no objection. 'Ring Nevsky and ask him, in my name, to prepare a special train for you. Be certain to take with you a couple of carriages manned by sailors, with a machine-gun. Between Kozlov and Tsaritsyn there is a dangerous situation.'

Vladimir Ilyich got to his feet and, sticking both his thumbs under the armpits of his waistcoat, went up to the map on the wall. I followed him.

'The Don Cossacks have cut the railway line. They've taken Aleksikovo . . .' And, quickly finding his bearings on the map, Vladimir Ilyich pointed out to me a station situated between Borisoglebsk and Serebryakovo station.

I was struck and deeply touched by the care that Vladimir Ilyich showed in not forgetting to warn me of the danger and in concerning himself with the protection I should have.

'And on the Volga there's a regular Vendée,' said Vladimir Ilyich bitterly, as he returned to his desk. 'I know the Volga countryside well. There are some tough kulaks there.' And, shaking his head, he sat down at the desk, on which books, documents, papers and forms were tidily arranged.

After a moment's pause, he said: 'Now, I'll write out a mandate for you. Today is Sunday and Bonch-Bruyevich isn't here. But that doesn't matter. You know where he lives? Go to his flat and get him to stamp this document.' Vladimir Ilyich vigorously shifted his chair closer to the desk, took up a form with on its top left corner the inscription: 'Chairman of the Council of People's Commissars of the RSFSR', and, bending his head low, wrote quickly.

'Well, there you are. I wish you success.' Vladimir Ilyich handed me my mandate.

I hastily read the document. Quite short, it testified that I

had been dispatched by the Council of People's Commissars to perform an urgent and important task at Novorossiisk, and, consequently, the authorities, civil, military and on the railway, were ordered to render me all possible assistance.

I thanked Vladimir Ilyich, lovingly shook his strong hand, and left the room.

Vladimir Dmitriyevich Bonch-Bruyevich, who was then in charge of the business of the Council of People's Commissars, was not to be found at his home. Returning to my flat, I telephoned the People's Commissar for Communications, Comrade V.I. Nevsky, and asked him to get a special train ready for me. Vladimir Ivanovich replied that everything would be seen to, and at 10p.m. sharp a special train consisting of a locomotive and one carriage would be waiting for me in Kazan Station.*

Accompanied by Altvater, I went by car to the Naval General Staff. Former Rear-Admiral Vasily Mikhailovich Altvater, with his big blue eyes and clipped beard like Nicholas II,† leapt up the steps and then mounted the wide staircase of the General Staff building, quickly and energetically, so that I, left behind and out of breath, could hardly keep up with him. When we got to his office Altvater asked for and handed over to me a thick, bound code-book and a long strip of paper on which were the encoding tables.§

II

Late that evening , as a persistent drizzle was falling, I arrived at Kazan Station. In the huge, dimly lit hall maintenance work was in progress. There was a stuffy, sour smell of wet clothes, *makhorka*** and sweat, and on the floor, on their bundles of belongings, amid a blue cloud of tobacco-smoke, lay the

---

* The station from which trains going eastward leave Moscow.

† Admiral V.M. Altvater (1883-1919), an officer of the Imperial Russian Navy, was at this time Assistant Chief of the Naval General Staff and a member of the Revolutionary War Council of the Republic.. Rumour had it that he was a natural son of Tsar Alexander III.

§ Probably a daily key, indicating where to enter into the code-book itself: a simple transcription code is greatly improved if the code changes every day.

** *Makhorka* is a cheap substitute for tobacco.

passengers, in overcoats and soldiers' greatcoats. I pushed on to
the brightly-lit platform, where the fresh evening air could be
breathed, and also the acrid smoke from the locomotives. On
one of the nearest tracks, beside a platform dark with rain,
stood a single blue carriage, with, in front of it, a locomotive
with steam up, making hoarse sounds, and in this a sooty
engine-driver in a black cap, leaning over the edge of the
fire-box, was letting off some hissing white steam.

I boarded the carriage, and the middle-aged station-master,
in his red cap, politely asked permission for the train to start.
We rushed away at a furious speed, making a wild, crazy
rumbling noise. My solitary carriage, its buffers and windows
jingling, creaked, rattled and shook: the well-sprung seat
bounced me, and my suitcases leapt about, as though possessed, in the string-netting rack.

In the morning, when I awoke, Ryazan was far behind us.
Soon the train pulled up at Kozlov. A military man came up to
me, in a tall black fur cap and a Caucasian jacket with silver
bullet-pouches and a short dagger in his belt.

'Tumarkin,' he said, smartly introducing himself, and, handing me a whole packet of tattered documents which he pulled
from his side pocket, asked if he might travel in my carriage. I
agreed. Comrade Tumarkin turned out to be a cavalryman
who was rejoining the front. He told me many interesting
things about the struggle between our Red Army men and the
Don Cossacks. From him I learnt that Aleksikovo station was
still in the hands of the Cossacks, so that he advised me to
proceed via Balashov to Kamyshin, from where I could carry
on by steamer down the Volga to Tsaritsyn. But such a detour
as this would take a lot of time. I decided to go by the direct
route, in the hope that that stretch of the railway line would be
clear of Krasnov's Cossack patrols by the time I got there.
While talking with Tumarkin I reached Gryazi station before I
had realised it. Here they warned me that the train could be
authorised to proceed no further than Borisoglebsk. Tumarkin
gave a sprightly salute, jingled his silver spurs, and leapt out on

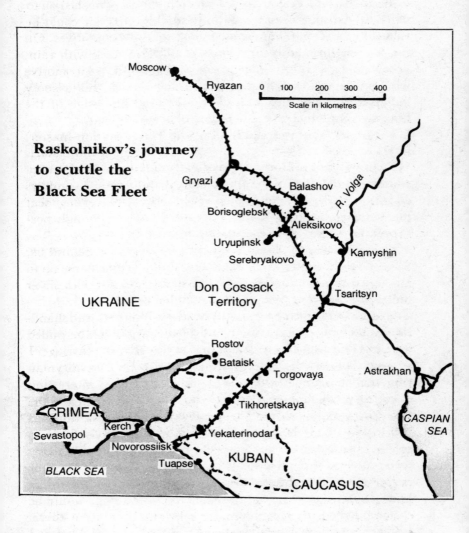

Moscow
Ryazan

0   100   200   300   400
Scale in kilometres

**Raskolnikov's journey
to scuttle the
Black Sea Fleet**

Gryazi
Balashov
R. Volga
Borisoglebsk
Aleksikovo
Uryupinsk
Serebryakovo
Kamyshin

Don Cossack
Territory

Tsaritsyn

UKRAINE

Rostov
Bataisk
Torgovaya
Astrakhan

Tikhoretskaya

CRIMEA
Kerch
Sevastopol
Yekaterinodar
CASPIAN
SEA

Novorossiisk
KUBAN

Tuapse

BLACK SEA
CAUCASUS

to the platform. Less than a year later I met him in Kirov's office at Astrakhan and was quite unable to recognise him. Instead of a strong, handsome young man there stood before me, leaning unsteadily on wooden crutches, a cripple who had become old and thin. When he saw me he smiled, cordially but with embarrassment. Brave Tumarkin had been riddled with bullets during a battle, but his heroic courage had not deserted him: he complained of the boredom of hospital life and with all his heart and soul yearned to be at the front again, in his own warlike element.

Before we got to Borisoglebsk the train halted at some little station. At the door of the single-storey station building hung, all by itself, a brass bell with a piece of rope, crudely knotted at the end, fastened to its clapper. I got out to stretch my legs on the platform. Not far from the station, beside a barn with a roof of rotten, blackened planks, I saw a crowd of people standing in a half-circle around some sort of lump. I quickened my steps till I reached this group. They parted slightly, making room for me. On a mound of wet, stinking mud lay a half-naked corpse. The deep-sunk, glassy eyes of the dead man were wide open, his thin, waxen nose was pointed, and a deathly pallor covered his face. His reddish hair had been clipped short, in the special way in which soldiers' heads were shaved in the Tsarist Army. His thin, bony chest and sunken belly were bare. In the upper part of his belly, which was yellow like wax, there was a small, round hole, surrounded by black, congealed blood. His legs and the lower part of his belly were covered with government-issue soldiers' trousers, but his feet were roughly wrapped in dirty, torn puttees: the dead man had no boots on. The decomposing corpse gave off a slight, barely perceptible sweetish smell of putrefaction.

'He pinched three roubles from a comrade. So they settled his account. How can anybody steal from a comrade?' said a young soldier in a service-cap and a blouse belted with a strap. And he explained that the murdered soldier, who had been demobilised, was returning home from the front, going back to his native village along with other soldiers: in the railway carriage he had stolen a green three-rouble note from one of his fellows, but had been caught in the act, and his comrades had stabbed him to death with their bayonets on the spot.

This was the last victim of the belated demobilisation of the disintegrated army of the dethroned Tsar. In the disciplined Red Army, which was being formed at that time, and was being tempered in the heat of battle like steel in fire, there were already no such lynchings any more, nor could there be.*

The peasants in their overcoats and the peasant women in their dark shawls who had gathered round the half-naked corpse sighed sorrowfully, exchanged glances and shook their heads. To none of them did it seem strange that a man's body should have lain for several days, like so much dung, in sunshine and rain, on a mess of liquid mud, and nobody, nobody at all, troubled to bury him.

III

I was not allowed to proceed beyond Borisoglebsk as a fierce battle was raging near Aleksikovo Station. Restless and anxious, I paced the boards of the platform, wet from recent rain. This unwanted delay greatly worried me. Every hour was terribly precious: I had to find the fleet at Novorossiisk, before it had upped anchor and gone off to Sebastopol. This forced halt at Borisoglebsk might ruin everything. Fortunately, I lost only a few hours. It was soon reported that the heroic Red Army men, led by Sievers and Petrov, had driven the Cossacks from Aleksikovo and cleared the railway. My train was the first to set off after the line had been reopened.

At Aleksikovo a traffic-jam had formed: all the tracks were blocked by green passenger carriages and dark-red heated goods-wagons, densely packed with people. Trains were being

---

* The 1936 edition omits the words 'nor could there be'. These are restored in the 1964 edition.

dispatched, in both directions, as their turn came. I went to see the man in charge of the station. In a dark little room, lit only by one dim window, the modest, good-looking station-master sat at his desk, wearing a threadbare double-breasted jacket. Facing him, sprawled on a chair, with his long legs, which were cased in high leather boots, stretched out in front of him, sat a young man who looked like a student, with a black, closely-clipped moustache and a bluish stubble on his pink young cheeks. I asked the station-master to let my train have first priority.   .

'My train is going first,' said the youngster, interrupting me in a free-and-easy way. 'I'm taking urgent medical supplies to the front.'

'I, too, have an urgent assignment, and can't afford to lose any time,' I said, and displayed the document Lenin had written out for me. Vladimir Ilyich's signature evidently produced its effect on the medical commissar. Instinctively, he straightened his legs: a pleasant expression brightened up his face, and he amiably suggested that we make up one single special train between us.

'How big is your train?' I asked.

'Two goods wagons laden with medical supplies. I'm taking them to Tikhoretskaya,' the student replied in a conciliatory tone.

Two additional carriages would not reduce the speed at which I travelled, and I agreed to combine our trains. The station-master, delighted with this solution of the problem, hurried off, brandishing his staff, to give the necessary orders. While the combined train was being made up I went into a siding packed with heavy carriages, to find Comrade Sievers's command post. I had no business to discuss with him. I just wanted to see Sievers and learn from him about the situation at the front. After wandering around for some time among the slippery sleepers I at last had pointed out to me a certain carriage which differed in no way from the others. I looked around for a sentry but could see none. Grasping the iron handrail I leapt nimbly on to the step, which was placed high above ground level, and knocked on the glass door. Sievers's *aide-de-camp* appeared on the platform clad in a neat military blouse gathered at the waist. He told me, politely, that Comrade Sievers was sleeping after some restless nights and exhausting military operations.

'However, if it's very necessary for you to speak to him, I'll wake him up.' I strongly objected to this proposal, asked that my greetings be conveyed to Comrade Sievers when he woke up, and, after shaking the hand of the slim, smart *aide-de-camp*, I jumped to the ground.

I had made the acquaintance of ex-Ensign Sievers, the editor of *Okopnaya Pravda (Trench Truth)*, in the Kresty prison, after the July days,* and had at once conceived a great liking for him. Frank, sanguine, militant, with a pink flush on his thin, hollow cheeks and inflamed eyes of bright blue, he, who came from the alien class of the Baltic-German landlords, had firmly linked his fate with the workers' revolution, and eventually died at the front, from typhus. Knowing neither fatigue nor rest, he constantly organised and led into battle troop after troop of Red Guards and, later, of Red Army men. A talented commander of large Red Army formations and a fearless fighter, he, like Kikvidze and Azin, perished just as his vital forces were coming into flower, and had no opportunity to develop all the gifts with which nature had generously endowed him.

When I got back to my own carriage, another local commander called on me in my compartment — Comrade Petrov. He had a short beard and his sunburnt face was tied round with white cheesecloth, under a tall black fur cap: from head to foot he was swathed in machine-gun belts. A man of middling height and broad-shouldered, with a low, hoarse voice, he was distinguished by iron energy and indomitable will-power. Cautiously seating himself on the edge of the springy, velvet-covered seat and holding a yellow leather whip in his hand, he

---

* See *Kronstadt and Petrograd in 1917*, pp.236-238.

told me that the Cossacks had withdrawn to Uryupinsk station, and that Comrade Kikvidze was tirelessly pursuing them with his guerrilla detachments. A few months later Petrov was arrested in Baku, sent off to India by the British, and shot, as one of the 26 Commissars, by the British Major Teague Jones.

The station-master asked if it was all right to despatch the train, and I said it was. Out of boredom the medical commissar moved into my compartment. A student at the Army Medical Academy, he had been sent from the front to obtain medical supplies, had procured some, not without difficulty, in Moscow, and now, guarding them like ingots of gold, was solicitously escorting them to his unit.

At Serebryakovo station I was met by the local military commissar, a robust and lively man in pince-nez and a black leather jacket. He told me that the station was on a war footing and ready to repulse immediately the expected raid by White Cossacks.

Suddenly, as happens in the South, the brief twilight gave place to sepulchral darkness.

IV*

Early next day the train reached Tsaritsyn. Among the endless parallel tracks near the station I sought out Comrade Stalin's carriage. He received me at once. A map was spread out on his desk. In a black high-collared jacket and trousers tucked into the tops of his high leather boots, his long, upstanding black

---

* As might be expected, there are interesting differences between the three editions where this section is concerned. In the 1936 edition Stalin does not 'stride towards' Raskolnikov to greet him, nor does he tell him he can catch up with Shlyapnikov at Torgovaya. In the 1964 edition everything between 'A map was spread out on his desk' and 'the categorical orders issued by the central authority in Moscow' is omitted, and also everything between 'Stalin shrugged his shoulders' and 'enormously helped me in the fulfilment of my task'. The editor of the 1964 version (which was published by the press of the USSR Ministry of Defence) appends a note stating that the Council of People's Commissars had ordered Stalin to see to the scuttling of the Black Sea Fleet, but he had replied, on June 15 1918, that he did not consider it appropriate for him to go in person to Novorossiisk, and he had sent Shlyapnikov instead. 'Thus, Stalin, evading fulfilment of a difficult and dangerous order, had sent, instead of himself, a man who, as he himself admitted, was "against scuttling the Black Sea Fleet".'

hair brushed back, and on his energetic face a thick, drooping moustache, Iosif Vissarionovich strode towards me and, taking his smoking pipe from his mouth with his left hand, stretched out his right hand.

Stalin was everything in Tsaritsyn: the Central Committee's plenipotentiary, a member of the Revolutionary War Council, the director of all Party and Soviet activity. As ever, he settled all problems collectively, in close contact with the local institutions, which impressed them and enhanced still further his unquestionable authority.

Stalin proposed that we sit down at his desk, and I then told him about the task that had been entrusted to me. I was astonished when I found that Stalin already knew all about it: about the to-ings and fro-ings of the struggle at Novorossiisk between advocates and opponents of the scuttling of the fleet, about the resistance put up by the leaders of the Black Sea-Kuban Republic,* and about the categorical orders issued by the central authority in Moscow.†

'A day or two ago Shlyapnikov passed through here,' said Iosif Vissarionovich, in a scornful tone. 'He, too, is against scuttling the Black Sea fleet. He doesn't understand.' Stalin shrugged his shoulders, turned his pipe over, and, sticking his forefinger into the bowl, slowly emptied the ashes into the

---

* In the early months of the Bolshevik Revolution several separate Soviet republics were set up in different parts of Russia. In North Caucasia there were four: Terek, Kuban, Stavropol and 'Black Sea'. The last-named, which covered the narrow coastal strip which includes Novorossiisk and Tuapse, merged with Kuban in May 1918. All these republics were united in July 1918 as the North-Caucasian Soviet Republic.

† For the 'disinformation' of the Germans, the Council of People's Commissars, after initially ordering that the fleet be scuttled, had sent, in clear, an order to return the ships to Sebastopol — accompanied by a message in cipher confirming the earlier order to scuttle. According to V.A. Kukel's account of this affair, Glebov-Avilov, the commissar of the Black Sea Fleet, at first tried to conceal the cipher telegram, but without success. He also says that Rubin, representing the Black-Sea-Kuban Republic, came to Novorossiisk on June 14 and made a speech threatening reprisals if the fleet were scuttled. Rubin claimed that his army was holding the Germans back, so that there was no immediate danger from them. Soon afterward, however, the Germans made a landing on the Taman Peninsula, which greatly worsened the military situation.

Stalin in 1918

ashtray: then, pulling his tobacco pouch towards him, he slowly unfastened it and refilled the pipe with small pinches of tobacco.

'Shlyapnikov is now at Torgovaya. You'll catch up with him,' Stalin added after a pause, having first lit a match, rekindled his pipe with profound concentration, and drawn deeply upon it. Lines gathered on his brow for a moment. Iosif Vissarionovich pointed out to me the mistake made by Vakhrameyev, who, having arrived at Novorossiisk with a definite directive from the Council of People's Commissars, concealed this for a long time from the leading Party comrades in the Black Sea-Kuban Republic.

'This ultra-conspiratorial behaviour never pays off,' he said, glancing at me with his kindly dark eyes and, wrinkling up his nose, he laughed a pleasant, throaty laugh. He advised me when I passed through Yekaterinodar, to call without fail upon the local leading comrades, to acquaint them with the purpose of my journey and secure their co-operation.

The moral support of Comrade Stalin and his concrete instructions enormously helped me in the fulfilment of my task. After taking leave of him, I returned to my own carriage and, within a few minutes, gently rocked by the springs, I was being conveyed further toward the South.

V

After I had left Tsaritsyn I noticed that we were being caught up by a train on the same track. It surprised me greatly that two trains should have been sent to follow each other in this way like trams on a tram-line. Never before or since did I see such a strange breach of railway procedure.

Beyond Tsaritsyn the situation was uncertain. Cossack patrols were moving about in the vicinity of the track and the stations were tensely awaiting raids. On the platforms stood narrow-barrelled Colt machine-guns, pointing towards the steppe. On the horizon the silhouettes of single horsemen stood out sharply. Against the pink evening sky their rifles stuck up like long, thin needles.

Along the high iron footboard, clutching the slippery hand-rail, I scrambled into the hot oily locomotive. The engine-driver, wearing a greasy leather apron, his face so blackened that his eyes looked big, like a Negro's, and his eyelids laden with soot, nodded amiably in reply to my request to ride on the locomotive. After wiping his hands on a greasy rag, he chucked it briskly into a far corner. The fireman noisily opened the door of the firebox and I was enveloped in unbearable heat. The engine-driver turned the regulator and a sharp, penetrating whistle followed. Laughing, I covered my ears, and went to stand on the buffer-beam, in front of the wide chimney. The medical commissar came and stood beside me. Puffing, the train moved slowly and smoothly out of the station. Gradually gathering speed, the wheels rattled faster and faster along the rails, the rhythm of their metallic clatter constantly quickening. Our little train was travelling at 60 kilometres an hour. A powerful, warm breeze blew against my face. The steppes — level, grey, boundless, smelling of flowers and grass — stretched away into the far distance. How pleasant it was to breathe the air of the steppes and enjoy the scenery which, though monotonous, was nevertheless fascinating, from the front of a fiery, rushing locomotive.

At the stations bareheaded women and children with naked, mouse-coloured feet offered us red boiled crabs.

Next morning we reached Tikhoretskaya, where there was some sort of headquarters. I entered their carriage and was received by the commander, an elderly man with close-cropped hair and a neatly trimmed black beard streaked with silver. From his upright and dignified figure one could guess with confidence that he was a former officer. 'Probably a colonel in the old army,' I thought. The commander told me that our forces were ten kilometres from Bataisk. They were opposed by Germans and also by units made up of Russian officers and Cossacks. In his opinion he could have taken Bataisk, and then Rostov, if only he had had sufficient artillery. But the material supplies of the Red Army on his sector of the front were at that time far from adequate. He changed the subject of our conversation to the struggle to scuttle the Black Sea Fleet. I told him nothing about the purpose of my journey, but he guessed it.

'Look here,' he said, 'if you scuttle the Black Sea Fleet I won't let you return.' He spoke these words in a grave tone, without the ghost of smile on his firmly-compressed lips: but his eyes gleamed with irrepressible goodwill.

I composed a telegram to Moscow, put it into code and handed it in at the railway telegraph office.

VI*

I arrived at Yekaterinodar that same day. I went into the stationmaster's office and asked him to provide me with a locomotive.

'I don't know whether I can send you on any further,' answered the elderly railwayman in the cap with a bright crimson top, in an ungracious tone. I gave my name.

---

* In this section, as in section IV, there are some interesting changes between editions. In the 1936 edition all mentions of Shlyapnikov are omitted, and also the mentions of Ostrovskaya, Gaven and Danilov. These are restored in the 1964 edition. The phrase 'In accordance with Comrade Stalin's advice' is omitted in the 1964 edition.

'People's Commissars are travelling around a lot too much,' he muttered, unwillingly. 'Mekhonoshin's just been through. Shlyapnikov is here, in a siding; and now you.'

I resorted to the ultimate measure, the document written by Vladimir Ilyich. Lenin's signature had a magical effect, and the stationmaster, sighing over the need to provide transport for both Shlyapnikov and me, promised to have a locomotive ready by the evening.

At the Executive Committee of the Black-Sea-Kuban Republic I met the local leaders, Ostrovskaya and Rubin.

The former, a short, sharp-faced brunette, had previously worked in Sebastopol and had enjoyed, along with Gaven and other Bolsheviks, very great influence in the Black Sea Fleet. She and Rubin were interested to know the views of the centre as to what was to be done with the fleet.

In accordance with Comrade Stalin's advice I explained our position to them with complete frankness, and also the purpose of my journey to Novorossiisk. They favoured armed resistance by the Black Sea Fleet to any German attack. I pointed out that the fleet could not operate without a base, and this base, Novorossiisk, was directly threatened by German land forces.

There had just been a German landing on the Taman Peninsula. A detachment of cyclists might at any moment appear on the railway line and cut Novorossiisk off from Yekaterinodar. Eventually, Ostrovskaya and Rubin reluctantly agreed that we had no alternative but to scuttle the Black Sea Fleet.

At the Executive Committee's premises I met Shlyapnikov, and we had a meal together. The rays of the sun flooded with their brilliant light a street that was fringed with green gardens. The leaves of the trees quivered under the light breath of a breeze. We went into a two-storeyed restaurant surrounded by a big garden, mounted the wooden staircase to the upper floor and sat down on an open veranda under the thick boughs of tall lime-trees with big dark boles. The air was heavy with the scent of fresh, sun-warmed leaves. Shlyapnikov, stout and thickset, with a small, closely-trimmed moustache, removed his soft felt hat with a sweeping gesture and placed it on the edge of the table. He was in a good mood. Speaking in his Vladimir accent,* he said, half-jokingly: 'Well, now, suppose they throw you overboard?' He was not in favour of scuttling the fleet. I remembered Comrade Stalin's warning. After a vegetarian meal we went to the station.

My train was soon ready. Ostrovskaya and Rubin saw me off. This was my first and last meeting with Rubin. Soon afterward, this robust and likable worker was shot by the adventurer Sorokin.

The southern darkness soon descended. Late in the evening, at Tonnelnaya station, I came upon Vakhrameyev's special train. On entering the carriage I found Vakhrameyev, Glebov-Avilov, Danilov and one other responsible executive from Novorossiisk.

'Where do you think you're going?' the red-whiskered Vakhrameyev asked me, with a worried look. 'They'll be waiting for you at the station, and they'll shoot you, that's for sure. They hunted us all through the town, and we barely managed to get out.'

'You'd much better go back with us to Yekaterinodar,' Glebov-Avilov advised me gloomily, wiping his spectacles with a handkerchief. 'There's a direct wire from there and we'll telegraph the order to scuttle the fleet.'

I replied, ironically, that in that case there would have been no need to leave Moscow, since there was a direct wire from Moscow to Novorossiisk, by which the order could just as well have been sent. Vakhrameyev shrugged. Glebov-Avilov stopped cleaning his glasses and stared at me from under his brows. 'We've got a crazy fellow here' was what I read in his astonished gaze.

Stepan Stepanovich Danilov, pale, thin and wearing pince-nez, with the hollow cheeks of a sick man and a pointed Don-

---

* Vladimir is to the east of Moscow, near the River Oka: the local people's pronunciation of the unstressed 'o' sounds comical to other Russians.

Quixote beard, sat morosely in the corner by the window and, except for coughing, observed the silence of the grave.

VII

I arrived at Novorossiisk early next morning and at once made my way to the harbour. The cloudless blue sky seemed infinitely high. The sun had not yet risen. A thin strip of summer dawn showed pink on the pale horizon. Frenzied, feverish activity was in progress in the unusually busy harbour. The quick, hasty movements of the railwaymen, dockers and sailors betrayed, however obscurely, the vague anxiety they felt. On the ships that lay by the landing-stage windlasses and winches rattled with a sound of exasperation, chain-cables clanked fitfully, and the regulators of steam-engines banged abruptly and loudly. Railway flatcars were being hurriedly loaded with small steam-launches with bright, coppery-yellow funnels, motor-destroyers with slightly raised bows, and grey guns taken from the ships, standing on their clumsy conical carriages, on the lower edges of which gaped the holes where the screws had been that fastened them to the deck. Sailors went by, straining under the weight of big bundles and with rifles slung across their backs. In the roadstead lay the grey sea-giant *Svobodnaya Rossiya*. Some pale smoke streamed almost imperceptibly from her wide, mighty funnels. Near the stone sea-wall lay some destroyers. Over a swaying gangplank I boarded the nearest of these, *Kerch*. Barefoot and sunburnt sailors, their working shirts hanging out and their trousers rolled up to the knees, were scrubbing the deck. A powerful stream of cold water was noisily spurting from long canvas hoses.

In a few hours' time the destroyer was to be plunged to the bottom of the sea, but, meanwhile, she lived her normal, every-day life, and the crew's work, as laid down in the ship's schedule, was being carried on with the precision of a well-regulated clock. I gave my name and asked the officer of the watch to provide me with a vessel to take me to *Svobodnaya Rossiya*. A small motor-launch, rocking rhythmically on the water, snuggled close to the steel side of the destroyer. The officer of the watch put it at my disposal.

Hardly, however had I left *Kerch* than a loud voice rang out from her deck: 'Comrade Raskolnikov, the commander wishes to see you.' I ordered that the launch be turned back, and climbed the ladder into the destroyer.

A rather thin man with a narrow, prominent nose on his tense face came up to me, wearing a white jacket and white, work-stained trousers. 'I am Kukel, the commander of this destroyer,' he said, politely introducing himself and raising his hand in salute to his badly-crumpled officer's cap. Wiping some big drops of sweat from his high, bulging forehead, Vladimir Andreyevich told me, speaking quickly and excitedly, about the events of the night that had just ended. It emerged that a few ships, led by the warship *Volya*, in which Tikhmenev flew his flag, had weighed anchor during the night and sailed away to surrender to the Germans.* When this squadron formed up in the outer roadstead, *Kerch* flew from her foremast a signal which read: 'To the ships going to Sebastopol. Shame on you traitors to Russia!'

'Isn't it possible to catch up with them and force them to return?' I asked. He pondered for a moment. 'It's too late now, alas,' he replied, after making a quick mental calculation. 'Tikhmenev will have reached Sebastopol before we could

---

* Captain A. I Tikhmenyev took over as acting commander-in-chief of the Black Sea Fleet after Admiral Sablin left for Moscow. On June 16 he carried out a referendum among the ships' companies. According to the White-Guard Captain N. Monasterev, 900 men voted to return to Sebastopol, 450 favoured scuttling, and 1,000 abstained. Kukel says that some of the last group advocated putting up a fight against the Germans, as a third option. He also claims that only 500 voted for returning to Sebastopol. Tikhmenyev took away one dreadnought, six destroyers and one auxiliary cruiser. These ships were eventually seized by the French interventionist forces and taken to the naval base at Bizerta, in Tunisia. The editor of the 1964 edition quotes S. M. Lepetenko, who took part in the scuttling, as saying that if Raskolnikov, with his authority among the sailors and his distinctive combination of vigour and tact, had arrived even one day earlier, the departure of some of the ships could have been prevented and the entire fleet scuttled.

overtake him. Besides, none of our crews are up to strength.'

Vladimir Andreyevich added that a desperate struggle was under way on all the ships, between advocates and opponents of the exodus to Sebastopol. *Svobodnaya Rossiya* had got up steam and prepared to weigh anchor. She would have left already but for shortage of men. The crew of *Kerch* had decided that in any case they would not surrender her and were ready to send the destroyer to the bottom. I warmly encouraged him in his commendable intention and promised him every support.

By chance I encountered on *Kerch* a cheerful, fresh-cheeked fellow named Deppish, who had been a class-mate of mine in the cadet training school: he was serving in the destroyer *Pronzitelny*. He came up and greeted me with a smile, revealing beneath his short, black, upward-twisted moustaches an even row of firm, white young teeth.

'I've just placed some good six-pound charges under the engine-cylinders,' he boasted smilingly, with a proud sense of moral satisfaction in the big and responsible task he had performed. Deppish was a fervent supporter of the plan to scuttle the fleet.

After once more voicing my approval and encouragement to Kukel, I got back into the launch and sailed across to *Svobodnaya Rossiya*. Hastily adjusting my blue naval jacket with its bright buttons, I hurried up the long ladder on to the warship's deck. To my surprise there was nobody on guard. The spacious deck was thronged with animated groups of sailors who were gesticulating with excitement and heatedly debating what to do.

Some sailors, wearing caps with the ribbons of St George and short black pea-jackets, were lugging huge bundles with both hands, straining at the weight, and then, with relief, stacking them near the ladder. They were preparing to abandon ship and go ashore. I asked someone to call the commander. Up came a clean-shaven seaman with light-red hair and a weatherbeaten, sunburnt face: he was wearing an off-white jacket, off-white trousers and off-white canvas shoes. After greeting me, Terentyev, as the commander was called, invited me into his cabin. Attracting the attention of the sailors, who stepped aside and made way for us, we walked across the wooden planking of the deck, which was as level and smooth as a tennis court. The anti-Soviet-minded engineer, Berg, growled after me some swear-word which I could not quite catch.

Terentyev and I descended a long ladder and found ourselves in the splendid, oak-pannelled and comfortably-furnished drawing-room of the Admiral's quarters. We sat down in big round chairs beside an elegant piano made of ebony, with bronze candlesticks at the corners. The commander listened attentively to what I had to tell him. He did not object to scuttling, but complained of the shortage of men and, in particular, of engine-room staff. I asked him to assemble all the sailors so that I could explain the task before us. Terentyev pressed a bell-push and told the orderly who came in reply to sound assembly.

On the top deck, under the long barrels of the 12-inch guns which looked like gigantic cigarettes, the sailors gathered, in their white duck-blouses with blue-and-white turn-down collars. Some, who came straight from work, were wearing striped vests, which made them look like zebras.

I made a fiery speech to the assembled men, describing the international situation of our Soviet country, and explained the absolute hopelessness of the position of the Black Sea Fleet.

'In order that the fleet may not fall into the hands of German imperialism and may not become a weapon of counter-revolution, we must scuttle it today.'

'But why can't we put up a fight, seeing that we have such splendid ships and such long-range guns?' a young sailor with feverishly burning eyes interrupted me to demand.

While agreeing that the ships were indeed splendid, I explained that the fleet could not operate without a base, and its only base, Novorossiisk, was threatened from the landward side. I pointed out that one ought not to see things from a parochial point of view. I reminded them that the forces of German imperialism had taken Narva and Pskov, and from these points would be able, if the war were resumed, to strike at Petrograd and even capture it. If the Black Sea Fleet began warlike operations, it would mean resuming the war with Germany, and for that we were not at the moment ready. Consequently, since we were unable to fight and did not want to go to Sebastopol and make a present of our ships to German imperialism, there was no honourable course open to us but to scuttle the fleet.

Terentyev spoke after me. Taking off his cap and mechanically stroking his smoothly parted reddish hair, he backed my proposal. There were no objections. A forest of hands was raised in support. The crew took their decision unanimously. Sailors both young and old wept and with tears in their eyes exclaimed: 'We're going to scuttle our *Svobodnaya Rossiya!*'

VIII

The Communist Party had carried on serious and important work in the Black Sea Fleet. The Party cells, which drew to themselves the best of the advanced sections of the active revolutionary sailors, functioned extensively on all the ships and wielded great influence. At Novorossiisk, however, the feeling among the sailors was complex and varied. The Communists there fully shared Moscow's view and were solidly in favour of scuttling. These were the basic cadres on whom the comrades carrying out the directive of the Council of People's Commissars could rely. But a considerable section of the Black Sea sailors held to the ultra-left theory of 'revolutionary war' and could not understand why it should be necessary to scuttle fine well-armed and battle-worthy ships. Their hearts yearned romantically for a beautiful death. Rather than scuttle the fleet they preferred to perish heroically. Unable to find their bearings in the complex international situation, they viewed it, so to speak, from the truck of their own ship. It seemed to them that the Black Sea Fleet ought to put to sea, bombard Sebastopol, which was occupied by the Germans, join battle with the German warships *Goeben* and *Breslau* and, after fighting to the

last shell, go down honourably in open naval combat. They were not troubled by what the consequences might be. They did not give any thought to the consideration that launching warlike operations in the Black Sea would mean violating the Brest Treaty and providing General Hoffmann and other champions of German imperialism with the excuse they wanted, to exploit their superiority of armed force and occupy Petrograd and Moscow. These harmful ultra-left inclinations of theirs brought the sailors theoretically close to the positions of the Left Communists and Left SRs, even though most of them had only the vaguest notions of Bukharin and Kamkov.

Among the crews, recruited as they were from workers and peasants, counter-revolutionaries were few and far between. But some backward elements did follow the lead of the reactionary officers and, by advocating departure to Sebastopol, objectively played a counter-revolutionary role. Some of the sailors had wives. Others, deceived by Tikhmenev, thought that by going to Sebastopol they would be loyally fulfilling the behest of the Council of People's Commissars. Finally, the cowards, quickly gathering up their belongings into big bundles, sacks and kitbags, hurried ashore, callously abandoning their ships to the mercy of fate. Counter-revolutionaries, provocateurs and German agents moved around the ships and the town, tempting and corrupting the sailors with propaganda, bribes and drink.

Among the former naval officers — titled aristrocrats and noblemen whose families were registered in the sixth velvet book* — the disgusting, loathsome counter-revolutionary opinion prevailed that 'the Germans are a lesser evil compared with Bolshevism'.

---

* Here Raskolnikov confuses two distinct genealogical reference works. The 'velvet book' was compiled in the 17th century, as a list of Russia's noble families. It was incomplete and, in any case, out-of-date by the 18th century, when a fresh classification was produced, dividing the nobility into six categories, with a separate book for each: the sixth book was devoted to the noble families of at least 100 years' standing, and included all the really old ones, such as the Sheremetevs, the Buturlins and the Golovins.

olshevik sailors at
azan, 1918

This worst section of the officers, who had lost all moral principles in the revolution, strove frenziedly to get to Sebastopol, which was occupied by German troops, so as to escape from 'Soviet hell'. Many officers wanted to go back to Sebastopol because their families, whom they had not managed to evacuate, were still there. In the depths of their hearts they realised that by surrendering their ships to German imperialism, and thereby strengthening its armed might, they were doing something base, vile and ignoble, which could not be described otherwise than as treason, but they put their personal and family interests before those of the proletarian state.

Another section of the officers considered it shameful to hand the fleet over to Germany, and declared for scuttling because of a feeling, inculcated from childhood and intensified by the long-drawn-out imperialist war, of traditional patriotism, with a marked nuance of anti-German chauvinism. Only a small group of energetic men among the junior officers stood consciously and wholeheartedly, along with the Communist vanguard of the Red Navy crews, for scuttling the fleet so that it should not fall into the hands of *any* imperialist country.

Fierce class struggle was fought on every ship. Advocates and opponents of scuttling argued day after day, foaming at the mouth, in the bunks and locker-rooms of every crew's quarters, and at the table of every wardroom. Meetings, delegate conferences, sessions of ships' committees assumed a permanent character. But the time for words had passed and the time for action had come.

IX

The motor-launch moved lightly away from the dreadnought and conveyed Terentyev and me to the shore. With a hard, metallic knocking of its piston, carried resoundingly across the water, the engine, puffing heavily and giving convulsive outbursts, worked loudly and fast, like a sluggish, dilated heart suffering from some incurable disease.

When we got to the quay we hailed a cab, and, seated in this narrow vehicle, made our way to the maritime transport office. As it rumbled along, the springless droshky raised great clouds of dust in its wake. The morning sunshine scorched our backs mercilessly. Terentyev took off his white-covered cap and used it to fan his sweaty, weatherbeaten face which was sunburnt, furrowed with wrinkles and covered with reddish freckles. The round-shouldered driver, wearing a torn cap, morosely called his thin, underfed nag to a halt in front of the entrance to a two-storeyed wooden house. We mounted a narrow, steep staircase. In a modest room furnished with desks and decorated with portraits of our leaders, we found the man in charge, and asked him to provide us with tugs.

'The fact is, comrades,' he said sadly, spreading his hands in a helpless gesture, 'we have tugs but not the men to operate them. Nearly all the crews have run away.' And he advised us to go to another institution of the merchant navy, where they also had some tugboats.

Terentyev excused himself for having to leave me. 'I must get the ship ready for scuttling and at the same time collect my things — I haven't packed them up yet,' he said cheerfully, and waving his cap, he went off with a confident and consequential air, towards the quay, taking wide strides with his strong, muscular legs in their roomy white trousers. I went on my own and on foot to the office indicated. The document written by Vladimir Ilyich exerted once again its magical effect. A tug was supplied for taking *Svobodnaya Rossiya* out of harbour.

Pleased with my success, I walked down the street. The initial tension had passed, and suddenly I felt an acute attack of extreme hunger. I turned into the first eating-house I came to — empty, dirty, with dusty windows that had not been cleaned for ages — and ordered lunch. I was given watery, muddy soup and, for the second course, tough, overdone meat. The stout elderly proprietress, with a protruding stomach and wearing a greasy cotton dress, offhandedly placed before me a pile of black bread. In Novorossiisk they had plenty of this.

When I had eaten, I went down to the harbour again. *Kerch* had already left the pier and was lying in the inner roadstead. I took a launch and went out to her. Kukel, his face pale, dirty with coal-dust, and all wet with sweat and fatigue, told me how the work was going. Powerful explosive charges had been placed in all the destroyers: they would be set off by lighting a Bickford fuse. The sea-cocks and scuttles had been opened and the covers torn off the portholes so that the water could rush in. I expressed my approval of the energetic measures Kukel had taken.

At this time the commander of the destroyer *Lieutenant Shestakov*, Anninsky, came across in a launch and boarded *Kerch*. The previous night he had got up steam and towed into the middle of the harbour the destroyer *Senior Lieutenant Baranov*, which almost all her crew had begun to abandon. About fifty men of a composite crew remained on *Shestakov*. Anninsky, short and cleanshaven, with the look of a sea-wolf, walked vigorously up to Kukel, who was bustling about the quarterdeck, from forecastle to poop, issuing curt orders and everywhere bringing bracing animation. After consulting with Kukel and receiving precise instructions from him, Anninsky hastened back in the launch to his own destroyer.

Kerch and *Lieutenant Shestakov* were the only vessels whose crews were up to strength and capable of towing other ships. On each of the remaining destroyers there were only five or six men left. Not even one man was left on the *Fidonisi*. That ship's commander, Mitskevich, had fled, under cover of darkness, the night before; he had rushed off in a launch to Kerch, and from there to Sebastopol.

I asked Kukel what his further intentions were. He replied that, after *Kerch* had completed her work at Novorossiisk, she would go to Tuapse, to be scuttled there. He explained that the reason for this move was that the crew of *Kerch* had from the very beginning openly stood for scuttling the fleet, and so had brought on themselves the particular displeasure of the Kuban people, and they were therefore afraid to pass through

Yekaterinodar. I considered this apprehension unfounded, but made no objection to the plan to scuttle *Kerch* at Tuapse.

Svobodnaya Rossiya was now approached by a small merchant steamer which looked, beside the dreadnought, like a child's toy. The steamer took the steel giant in tow and, furiously puffing smoke and straining hard, slowly dragged her into the outer roadstead.

Anninsky, sharply issuing orders from the high bridge of *Shestakov*, drew the destroyers out of the harbour. When one had been taken to the roadstead he returned at once for another.

The composite crew of the *Shestakov*, who shared with *Kerch* the principal role in preparing the scuttling operation, showed outstanding heroism. The overworked stokers, panting from the heat, stuffiness and effort, kept tirelessly at their task. The entire crew was brought to the point of exhaustion.

Soon after this an auxiliary-powered schooner, low in the water, moved away from the side of *Svobodnaya Rossiya*, fully laden with sailors taken from the warship. At the edge of the deck, his legs set wide in a graceful attitude, stood Terentyev, in an elegant snow-white suit.

When the schooner passed *Kerch*, as she lay in the roadstead, Terentyev shouted, loudly and gaily: 'Commander Kukel! There's an empty box for you, do what you like with it!' And he waved his freckled hand, covered with red hairs, in a contemptuous gesture towards *Svobodnaya Rossiya*.

X

When I reached the shore, the mole, the landing stage and the dusty quay were black with a dense crowd. The whole population of Novorossiisk had poured out on to the seashore. Men, women and children were huddled together, jostling each other. Near the cement works some workers stood by the shore, gazing sadly at the destruction of the ships. Many had climbed on to the white heaps of lime or on to the high embankment in order to have a better view of this unusual spectacle.

On the landing-stage, beside which lay *Fidonisi*, abandoned by her crew, an improvised meeting was in progress. A fervent speaker, who had clambered up a lamp-post and was firmly clinging to it with both legs and one hand, was despairingly waving his other hand in the air. In a quavering, hysterical voice he called on the crowd not to let the ships be scuttled. The speaker's appeal met with success. When the schooner which had come in from the roadstead started to take *Fidonisi* in tow, the crowd, which had been stirred up, tried to hold the destroyer back. *Kerch* put on speed and, briskly swinging round, approached the landing-stage. 'Action stations' was sounded on board the ship. Her terrible guns, aimed at the landing-stage, were got ready for action. Kukel, lean and intense, raised to his lips a megaphone like a funnel-shaped trumpet that gleamed in the sunshine, and shouted in a strained voice: 'If I am prevented from towing this destroyer away, I shall at once open fire.' The threat took effect. The crowd on the landing-stage immediately fell back, and *Fidonisi* was towed out into the roadstead.

At about four in the afternoon *Kerch* fired a Whitehead torpedo at the destroyer *Fidonisi*. There was a deafening explosion, the destroyer shook and everything was shrouded in a cloud of smoke. When the smoke-curtain had dispersed the destroyer was seen to be mutilated beyond recognition. The forward bridge had partly collapsed, the wheel house had been severely crumpled and damaged. Both masts, with their upper parts broken off, looked like trees whose tops had been lopped. Gradually the bow of the ship began to rise, and all at once the destroyer, having filled with water, went like a stone to the bottom. After that, the sea-cocks were opened in the others, and one by one the rest of the destroyers perished. The slanting rays of the setting sun lit up the dark shapes of the ships as they drowned beneath their red flags, with this signal hoisted: 'I perish, but I do not surrender.'

The workers who were watching this spectacle from the shore sighed and furtively wiped away the tears that welled up. From time to time the low, restrained sobbing of women could be heard. In the harbour, instead of the lively activity of a moment before, some thin masts projected dolefully out of the water. At half past four two torpedoes were fired from *Kerch* at *Svobodnaya Rossiya*. They splashed into the water and, cutting across the surface, leaving behind them a long, straight, transparent wake, rushed quickly towards the warship. One passed under the keel of *Svobodnaya Rossiya*, but the other exploded under the gun-turret at her bow. A column of black smoke rose from the water, hiding the ship's grey hull up to the level of the round conning-tower. Yet *Svobodnaya Rossiya* remained calmly afloat. *Kerch* fired a third torpedo. Even after this had exploded, however, the warship stayed where it was, as though nothing had happened. A fourth torpedo exploded under the turret at the stern, but even this produced no result. After three hits by powerful torpedoes, which had caused an immense conflagration, the ship was neither listing nor sinking. The floating armoured giant of 23,000 tons displacement seemed invulnerable, like a legendary dragon. The commander and crew of *Kerch* were in despair. Their stock of Whitehead torpedoes was running out. A fifth torpedo was fired. Before it reached *Svobodnaya Rossiya*, however, this one suddenly made a U-turn and came back. The destroyer began to manoeuvre so as to get out of the way of her own crazy torpedo, which, glistening like silver, was racing at lizard-like speed, directly at *Kerch*. Something had gone wrong in the aiming-mechanism of the torpedo. It was being drawn like a magnet to the steel hull of the destroyer, and changed course three times. Finally, after turning back towards *Svobodnaya Rossiya*, it suddenly leapt like a dolphin out of the water, broke in half, and sank at once. Another torpedo was fired, and this one, after falling flat on to the surface of the water, rushed towards *Svobodnaya Rossiya* and struck her right amidships. Dense white smoke rose up, completely enveloping the dreadnought. When the smoke dispersed, the vessel was unrecognisable: the thick armour covering her sides had been torn off in several places, and huge holes, with twisted leaves of iron and steel, gaped like lacerated wounds. Rocking from the explosion, the ship slowly heeled over to starboard. Then she began to turn upside down, with a deafening clang and roar. The steam-launches and lifeboats fell, smashed, rolled across the deck and, like so many nutshells dropped off the high ship's side into the water. The heavy round turrets, with their three 12-inch guns, broke from the deck and slid, making a frightful din, across the smooth wooden planking, sweeping away everything in their path and at last, with a deafening splash, fell into the sea, throwing up a gigantic column of water, like a waterspout. In a few moments the ship had turned right over. Lifting in the air her ugly keel, all covered with green slime, seaweed and mussels, she still floated for another half-hour on the grey-green water, like a dead whale. The red-clawed seagulls circled for a long time, scarcely moving their wings, over the shell of the upturned ship, like aeroplanes over the fresh grave of an airman who has crashed. Tall fountains spurted from the open sea-cocks and scuttles of the drowned vessel. Slowly and gradually the oblong, mis-shapen floating object shrank in size and at last, with a gurgling and a bubbling, was hidden beneath the waves, dragging with it into the deep great clouds of foam, and forming a deep, engulfing crater amid a violently seething whirlpool.

On the deck of *Kerch* the sailors, tense-faced and silent, as though at a funeral, bared their heads. Broken sighs and suppressed sobs could be heard.

'Slow speed ahead!' ordered Kukel briskly, from the bridge. *Kerch* swung round and then, at full speed, soon disappeared round a headland.

At dawn next day she was scuttled off Tuapse. Before being consigned to the depths of the sea the ship's wireless sent out this message: 'To all, to all, to all. I perish, after destroying those ships of the Black Sea Fleet that preferred death to shameful surrender to Germany. Destroyer *Kerch*.'

At seven that evening, when we gathered at the railway station to await the departure of our train, a German airplane circled over the town. We could make out the sinister black crosses on its yellow wings. After describing several wide circles over the empty harbour, the aeroplane, like a great bird of prey, spreading its long wings, flew back to Sebastopol to report to its masters the heroic fate of the Red fleet.*

* According to Monasterev one dreadnought and eleven destroyers were scuttled. Speaking at the Fourth Conference of Moscow's trade unions and factory committees on June 28 1918, Lenin said: 'I will reply to the question about the Black Sea Fleet, which seems to have been put for the purpose of exposing us. Let me tell you that the man who was operating there was Comrade Raskolnikov, whom the Moscow and Petrograd workers know very well because of the agitation and Party work he has carried on. Comrade Raskolnikov himself will be here and he will tell how he agitated in favour of destroying the fleet rather than allow the German troops to use it for the purpose of attacking Novorossiisk. That was the situation in regard to the Black Sea Fleet: and the People's Commissars Stalin, Shlyapnikov and Raskolnikov will arrive in Moscow soon and tell us all about it.' (*Collected Works*, Vol.27, pp.485-486).

Men in Matting

I

Three destroyers swam, like black swans, over the broad, high waters of the River Kama.* Carefully skirting the frequent sandbanks and shoals, keeping close now to the right, the higher bank, now to the left, the lower one, they hastened toward Red Sarapul, which had been taken by Comrade Azin's Iron Division.

The sharp iron stems of the narrow-built destroyers made a murmurous purling as they cut through the smooth, dark-blue water. They were in line-ahead formation, with *Prytky* leading, then *Prochny*, and *Retivy* bringing up the rear. The dark autumn night shrouded the river in impenetrable darkness. From time to time there was a flicker of reddish light from the villages on the banks. The steel hulls of the warships trembled silently. In the stuffy, dirty boiler-rooms the shirtless stokers, muscular as circus strong men, vigorously and deftly threw heavy shovelfuls of small coal into the open fire-chambers and, bathed in sweat, fed the fiery furnaces. Slowly and cautiously, the engineers poured warm, thick, heavy lubricant from the long, narrow necks of oil-cans on to the swiftly plunging pistons. After wiping their hands on greasy, black rags, with a confident air they turned small wheels and operated long, awkwardly protruding levers.

---

* At this time — October 1918 — all the waterways of the Volga-Kama basin had been placed by the Soviet Government under Raskolnikov's authority.

Rescue of the Men in Matting

VYATKA

PERM

R. Kama

VOTKINSK

IZHEVSK

GALYANI

NIKOLO-BEREZOVKA

AGRYZ

R. Volga

R. Byelaya

KAZAN

From
Moscow

R. Kama

CHISTOPOL

UFA

R. Volga

0   60   120
Scale in kilometres

SIMBIRSK

Beside me on the high bridge of the leading destroyer, grasping one of the spokes of the helm and peering out into the blackness, stood our navigator. He was an old pilot with a long, grey beard that reached to his waist, and wore a shabby black cap and a long-skirted overcoat, like an Old-Believer Bible-reader.*

'Couldn't you increase our speed, Grandad?' I asked him, impatiently.

'No, indeed, comrade commander,' the old man replied gloomily. 'This is a difficult reach, the buoys aren't alight and the night is dark. I don't know how we're going to get by.'

His serious tone and quavering voice betrayed uncertainty and anxiety. In all his many years as a pilot he had never before had to undertake such a risky voyage as this. We must at all costs get to Sarapul. Closely pursuing Admiral Stark's White-Guard flotilla, we had forced them to turn into the River Byelaya, blocked the mouth of that river with small, oblong whiskered mines of the 'Rybka' (Fish) type, and left almost all the vessels of our own flotilla behind to guard this minefield. The army commander, the energetic Shorin, had ordered the destroyers to break through to Sarapul and bring help to the Red land forces there. The large, rich, grain-trading village of Nikolo-Berezovka, which lay between us and our objective, was occupied by the Whites. On the bank near this village stood a battery of three-inch field guns. Consequently, we were going to be able to get through only by night, when conditions for navigating were extremely difficult. Fortunately, the waters of the Volga and the Kama were unusually high in 1918.

Amid the dense darkness golden sparks were flying from the destroyer's funnels and fiery-red columns blazed up from them. Through the speaking tube I told the stokers about this, and within a few minutes thick black smoke was pouring out of the wide, sloping funnels. We had to creep along quickly and

---

* Those members of the Russian Orthodox Church who refused to accept the reforms introduced by Patriarch Nikon in 1653-1676 broke away and were thereafter known as the 'Old Believers', or *raskolniki* (schismatics).

inconspicuously, lest the Whites should spot us and open fire. Our lights were extinguished. All the hatches were battened down and the portholes tightly closed with their heavy covers. None of the crew was smoking on deck. Those smokers who could not hold out had to go below, and in that stuffy atmosphere inhale their strong-smelling *makhorka*.

'We're getting near to Nikolo-Berezovka,' the pilot warned me in a half-whisper. On the right the huts of a sleeping village were dimly visible. In the strained and eerie silence the ship's engine was working dully and rhythmically like a great iron heart. Our speed caused the stern to quiver gently: behind it rose a frothy heap of water churned up by the blades of our screws. The deep silence of the sleeping village was suddenly broken by the loud, jerky barking of dogs. Just opposite Nikolo-Berezovka there was a steep, dangerous sandbank. Luckily, we managed to get round it all right. After that, the reach became less difficult, and we could use the middle of the river. A sigh of relief broke from the hollow chest of the old pilot when the dangerous place had been left behind. He lifted the shabby black cap from his grey head, turned up to the heavens his sad, grey eyes and, with a sweeping gesture, crossed himself, to the amazement of the smiling sailors.

II

All the authorities of Sarapul had assembled on the covered floating landing-stage, to greet our flotilla: the secretary of the local Party committee, the chairman of the executive committee of the soviet, the garrison commander and the commanding officer of a regiment. On the shore, in front of a throng of workers, a Red Army band, dressed in long grey overcoats, their brightly-polished brass trumpets gleaming in the sunshine, were playing a cheerful march. The destroyers, dragging behind them a long sheet of dark-brown smoke, passed under the high, still-unfinished railway bridge and were moored, one after the other, beside the crowded landing-stage.

The comrades who had come to meet us stepped forward, in their light sheepskin coats and black leather jackets, to introduce themselves and shake our hands.

'Where is Comrade Azin?' I asked, because I particularly wanted to meet him.

'He's at Agryz — that's where divisional headquarters is now,' they replied.

I clambered up a steep slope and made my way to the office of the local soviet, a two-storeyed stone house with a balcony, looking out on the dirty market square. In the tiny rooms, furnished with plain, unpainted wooden tables, some visitors, young workers from Izhevsk, were scurrying about. Members of the Soviet were patiently giving them the information they wanted.

A tarnished samovar bubbled in the small canteen, sending out a trickle of steam from the hole in the top. On the counter lay plates with slices of black bread and yellow Dutch cheese.

Sitting before a glass of hot tea I learnt that, not far from Sarapul, in the village of Galyany, some workers from Izhevsk who had been captured by the Whites were imprisoned on a barge and in danger of being shot. There were numerous Communists among them.*

'We must rescue them all,' I thought. However, the barge lay behind the White-Guard lines: the front ran between Sarapul and Galyany. This meant that we should have to get through into the enemy's rear, which would call for some military cunning. I hurried back to the ship. The Sarapul comrades shook our hands concernedly and wished us success.

---

* It is not clear whether these men were 'workers from Izhevsk'. The workers of the factories at Izhevsk and Votkinsk, who were under SR influence, had rebelled against the Soviet Government in August 1918, and joined the Whites. According to Larissa Reissner, who was with Raskolnikov on this voyage, the prisoners were Bolshevik sympathisers among the Sarapul population whom the Whites carried off with them when they withdrew from that town, and were being taken *to* Votkinsk. She mentions that there were several Chinese among them — presumably captured Red Army soldiers. Some of the prisoners may have been workers from Izhevsk and Votkinsk who, after serving in the 'People's Army' which the rebels had formed to fight against the Bolsheviks, had become disaffected and subjected to arrest for unreliability.

When I was once more on board *Prytky*, I gave this order to all three destroyers: 'Haul down the red flags.' Everyone was surprised, but obeyed unquestioningly. 'All hands on deck! Weigh anchor!' — the brisk command rang out, and everyone fell to.

At last the destroyers moved off, carefully detaching themselves from the landing-stage. We were going into battle. Our masts, bare like giant barge-poles, looked lonely without their flags.

Immediately beyond Sarapul, which occupied a fine position on the high bank, lay yellow fields of stubble and well-mowed meadows. Suddenly, ahead of us on the right bank, we observed a small group of armed men. This was the front line. Lying all alone on its side, on a shoal, was a black, tar-besmeared fishing boat. We drew near to the bank and, after switching off our engines, entered into conversation with the men in military uniform, who wore epaulettes.

'Who is the senior officer here?' demanded our officer of the watch through his megaphone, his manly voice ringing out over the quiet river.

From the group of soldiers stepped forward a thickset, broad-shouldered fellow in a neat, new khaki jacket and riding-breeches tucked into glossy leather boots.

'I am,' he replied in the usual smart military manner.

'And who are you?' came the voice, again, from our destroyer.

'Sergeant-Major Volkov,' was the brisk reply from the man on the bank, as he squared his broad shoulders.

'The fleet commander, Admiral Stark,' I said to the officer of the watch, who repeated my words through his megaphone, 'orders you immediately to come on board this destroyer.'

Sergeant-Major Volkov hesitated. After thinking for a moment, he went up to the fishing-boat and tried to launch it into the water, but then, suddenly, with a suspicious glance at the destroyer, like an animal scenting danger, he rushed back in the direction from which he had come. The Maxim gun on my

destroyer rattled loudly, firing at him as he ran, but he succeeded in taking cover behind a high, green mound.

The destroyers glided on further, quickly and smoothly,
cutting their way through the calm waters of the river.

III

To our left, on a hill, stood the white stone church of Galyany
village. Below the church, in the middle of the river, a blackened wooden barge lay at anchor. Sitting or standing on the
barge were armed men in black sheepskin coats and shaggy
caps. Beside the church a three-inch field gun showed grey, and
a machine-gun projected from the embrasure of the belfry. Not
far from the church a broad-beamed, clumsy-looking paddle-
steamer lay beside a landing-stage.

To the right of this, on the lower bank, from the bushes that
covered a sloping sandbank, soldiers in greenish jackets and
breeches tucked into high, tight-fitting leather boots were gazing at us with curiosity. The relaxed bearing of these soldiers,
standing with their hands in their pockets, was redolent of the
peaceful placidity of the rear.

When *Prytky* had drawn level with the floating prison, I
issued this command: 'His Excellency, Admiral Stark, orders
you to get ready. We are going to take this barge, with the
prisoners, in tow and bring it to Ufa.'

The morose faces of the guards beamed with pleasure. Pro-
ximity to the front evidently caused them anxiety, and the news
that they were to be moved into the deep rear was cheering to
these prison-warders.

'But what about the Reds?' one of them asked, uncertainly.
'They're at Sarapul, you know.'

'Sarapul was captured this morning by our valiant troops.
The Reds have fled to Agryz,' the officer of the watch replied
through his megaphone, following my instructions.

Joy shone from the faces of the guards. Evidently they had
been dreaming day and night of the capture of Sarapul by the

Whites and of moving to distant, secure Ufa, and so they easily, eagerly believed what I told them. They brightened up, assumed a dignified air, and, cheerfully bustling about and shouting, began, swiftly and deftly, to raise the heavy iron anchor by hand. My destroyer approached the paddle-tugboat that lay, all by itself, beside the landing-stage, laden with a small stack of birchwood.

Our young, ruddy-faced officer of the watch, with a soft down on his cheeks, lifted the megaphone to his lips and, prompted by me, shouted loudly and clearly: 'Tugboat!'

After a short pause a hoarse voice answered: 'Aye, aye!'

'By order of the fleet commander, Admiral Stark, you are to take in tow the barge with the prisoners and bring it to Ufa. We shall give you protection.'

'We haven't enough fuel,' an elderly native of the Volga country, with a a curly brown beard, answered from the bridge of the tugboat.

'That's all right, we'll pick some up on the way,' shouted back in an authoritative tone, through his megaphone, the former Sub-Lieutenant who had graduated from Naval College two years before.

'Aye, aye!' was the obedient reply from the tugboat's captain, and he briskly pushed off from the landing-stage, fastened a tow-rope to the barge, and began slowly pulling it along after his own vessel.

The White-Guard soldiers standing on the bank watched with calm curiosity the destroyers, the tugboat, the barge and all our manoeuvres. No danger was to be expected from them. All that I was afraid of was that the guards on the barge would, at the last moment, realise what was happening and, in desperation, would throw hand-grenades into the hold and blow up our imprisoned comrades.

However, the guards, suspecting nothing, sailed off on the prison-barge, which from that moment became their own prison. An elderly warder, sitting on a coil of thick rope, was peacefully and unconcernedly smoking his pipe. When *Prytky* drew alongside the barge, without getting up he took the pipe out of his mouth and gaily made a quick, rotatory movement with his arm, as though to say: 'Roll on faster, lads!'

The autumn twilight descended and the damp coolness of the river was felt in the air. In Sarapul a swarm of bright lights were shining. Under cover of darkness we passed unnoticed through the front line. On the deck of the dimly perceivable barge the guards' cigarettes were points of light like glow-worms.

Soon we arrived at the Sarapul landing-stage. The White-Guard prison-warders, taken by surprise, were arrested without difficulty and brought ashore.

In the depths of the dark and dirty hold, in a stinking, fetid atmosphere, huddled a company of half-naked men, barely covered by torn pieces of matting. How glad these captives were to have been set free! Many of the workers wept for joy, unable to believe their good luck.

The men we had saved from an agonising death numbered 453.

I asked the comrades to spend one last night on the barge, so that in the morning they could be given a ceremonial welcome in the town.

IV

The garrison commander asked me to come and see him. A brave, resolute man with a glass eye which made him seem to squint, he lived in a street in the centre of the town, in the flat of a bourgeois who had run away.

In his spacious and bright dining-room, furnished simply but with taste, before a glass of tea and to the soft humming of a cosily seething samovar, the garrison commander told me that Vladimir Aleksandrovich Antonov-Ovseyenko was now at Agryz and intended to be at Sarapul next day.*

---

* Antonov-Ovseyenko was at this time a member of the Supreme War Council.

Rescued prisoners on barge at Sarapul landing-stage

The slim young mistress of the flat, who dispensed our tea, told me with a naive air that her husband, an engineer who sympathised with the Whites, had fled with them to Ufa. She had wanted to leave with her husband, but they would not let her bring on to the barge in which the refugees were escaping the goat with long white hair and hooked nose which nourished with her milk this young woman's new-born daughter, and the mother could not go without her wet-nurse naïny-goat: the doctors had absolutely forbidden her to feed the child herself. For this reason she had stayed behind in Sarapul, and was very pleased when she found that the Bolsheviks were not at all as frightful as the terrified imagination of the philistines had depicted them. She soon forgot her husband, and consoled herself by becoming the wife of the garrison commander, who had by accident come to live in her flat. It is in ways like this that people's personal fate is sometimes determined.*

Early next morning, when the low sky was covered with leaden clouds that hung over the town, the great exodus began. Pale, emaciated, exhausted, half-naked, clutching to their chests some torn pieces of matting they had thrown round their shoulders, the released prisoners walked barefoot into the market square. Their naked bodies showed white through big rents in the matting that covered them. The men in matting made a long procession. The workers and craftsmen of Sarapul — tanners and cobblers — watched with sorrowful sympathy this sombre parade and emotionally waved their handkerchiefs. The sailors of the Red fleet greeted the liberated men with a welcoming 'Hurrah!' Women in coloured head-scarves turned away to wipe tears from their red, swollen eyes.

'There you see it, the uniform of the Constituent Assembly!'† was the bitter remark of someone in the crowd.

---

* The last two sentences, except for the words 'she soon forgot her husband' were omitted from the 1936 edition, but restored in that of 1964.

† The White forces on the Eastern front fought at this time under the banner of the Constituent Assembly, which they claimed to be the legitimate 'Parliament' of Russia, arbitrarily suppressed by the Bolsheviks.

A tribune of planks, with a railing, had been erected in the market square, and from this I delivered a short speech of greeting to the comrades we had freed. Other comrades spoke after me. No-one said much. The procession of barefooted men in matting spoke more strikingly and powerfully against the Whites than any inflammatory speech could have done.

In conclusion, one of the men in matting spoke, telling of the dreadful conditions on the prison-barge: he ended by saying that he was going to join the Red Army. Other ex-prisoners followed his example. Gripped by enthusiasm, the crowd warmly applauded their revolutionary impulse.

At the end of the meeting the men in matting were invited to take tea in a restaurant in the market square. Their faces shone with pleasure: they felt that they were men who had been in the jaws of death and had been restored to life. They had been given new hope. Hastily and joyfully they threw off their dirty, ragged matting and put on human clothes. Many of these workers went straight out of their matting into Red Army uniform and were immediately sent off to the front. On November 7 1918, the anniversary of the great proletarian October, the Izhevsk works was captured by Red troops after a violent assault.

Many of the 'barge-men' took part in this assault. Some of them met before Izhevsk the death of the brave, laying down their lives, which they had devoted to the revolution, for the well-being of the working class, for the Communist Party.*

---

* The raid on Galyany was carried out on October 17, 1918. On October 20 the three destroyers were sent to Astrakhan to reinforce the Bolsheviks' flotilla on the Caspian Sea.

A prisoner of the British

I

In Petrograd in December 1918 a persistent rumour circulated to the effect that some ships of the British navy had entered the Gulf of Finland. It was seriously alleged that a British naval squadron had arrived at Reval. However, since philistine tittle-tattle exceeded all bounds in those days, one had to treat every sensational story with the greatest caution.* Nobody knew for certain what the situation was. The Baltic Fleet command despatched submarines on several occasions to try and enter Reval harbour and make a thorough reconnaissance, but the poor technical condition of these vessels prevented them from fulfilling this assignment. Owing to defects in their mechanisms the submarines returned without completing their task. The reconnaissance mission of the submarine *Tur* commanded by Nikolai Aleksandrovich Kol also failed to get results.†

Then, one day, our wireless station intercepted some British messages asking for pilots to be sent from Reval: as, however, these messages were sent in clear, nobody ascribed any importance to them. They were interpreted as one of the usual tricks

---

* Following Germany's defeat in the West the Soviet Government repudiated the treaty of Brest-Litovsk and Red Army forces advanced into Estonia and Latvia, where 'bourgeois-nationalist' governments had been set up in the capitals — Reval (Tallinn) and Riga. A British squadron was sent to help the anti-Bolshevik forces, arriving at Reval on December 12, 1918.

† The sentence about the submarine *Tur* is omitted in the 1964 edition.

by the 'Allies' aimed at frightening our fleet and keeping it in Kronstadt harbour.

The German revolution which broke out on November 9 had resulted in the All-Russia Central Executive Committee annulling the peace treaty of Brest-Litovsk. Narva and Pskov had been taken by the Red Army. Only feeble resistance was put up by the German soldiers, and our men had had, in the main, to overcome units composed of Russian White-Guard officers.*

The Revolutionary War Council of the Republic decided to carry out a reconnaissance in depth to ascertain the strength of the British fleet in the Gulf of Finland. As a member of the Revolutionary War Council of the Republic I was appointed to take command of a special task-force. The day before our expedition, in the evening of December 24, a conference was held in the office of the commander of the Baltic Fleet, under the gilded spire of the Admiralty, to work out the plan for this operation. Present were V.M. Altvater,† Baltic Fleet Commander Zarubayev, his chief of staff Weiss, operations chief S.P. Blinov and myself.

Owing to the technical state of the ships, which were undergoing winter repairs, the Baltic Fleet command could assign only a small force for this operation. The battleship *Andrei Pervozvanny*, the cruiser *Oleg* and three destroyers of the *Novik* class, *Spartak* (formerly *Miklukho-Maklay*), *Avtroil* and *Azard* were all the vessels placed at my disposal. As we did not know the size of the British fleet which had penetrated into Baltic waters, we could not undertake to destroy the enemy completely. The participants in the conference at the Admiralty were united in concluding that my expedition could be ordered

---

* On Estonian territory there were, besides the local anti-Bolshevik forces, also a number of Russian 'Whites', who formed themselves into an army which was first commanded by General Rodzianko and later by General Yudenich.

† Admiral V.M. Altvater (1883-1919), an officer of the Imperial Russian Navy, was at this time Assistant Chief of the Naval General Staff and a member of the Revolutionary War Council of the Republic. Rumour had it that he was a natural son of Tsar Alexander III.

to carry out no more than a reconnaissance in depth, which might end in a fight to destroy the enemy only if it became clear that we possessed definite superiority over the British forces. On Comrade Altvater's initiative we unanimously adopted the following operational plan: *Andrei Pervozvanny*, under Zagulyaev's command, would remain in the rear, near the Shepelevsky Light fairly close to Kronstadt; the cruiser *Oleg*, under Saltanov's command, would advance to Hogland* Island; the two destroyers *Spartak* and *Avtroil* would penetrate Reval harbour, in order to discover how many British ships were there, and would open fire on Nargen and Wulf Islands,† so as to find out whether there were any batteries on these islands. If they encountered superior forces, the destroyers were to withdraw to Hogland, under the protection of *Oleg's* heavy guns, and in the event that this protection proved inadequate, all three vessels were to retreat eastward, to Kronstadt, luring the enemy toward the Shepelevsky Light where the 12-inch guns of *Andrei Pervozvanny* would be waiting for him. The conference thus laid the entire risk of the operation on the destroyers — which in case of danger, possessed the inestimable advantage of being able to make a speed of 30 knots.§

---

* Hogland is now usually shown on maps under its Finnish name, Suursaari.

† Nargen and Wulf are now usually shown on maps under their Estonian names, Naissaar and Aegna.

§ According to the *History of the Estonian SSR*, edited by G.I. Naan, published in Tallinn in 1952 (p.352): 'The myrmidons of American [*sic*] and British imperialism — the Trotskyists — were active in the Soviet rear. On 26-27 December 1918 Trotsky and his assistant Raskolnikov sent into the Gulf of Tallinn [Reval] where a British squadron was stationed, the destroyers *Spartak* and *Avtroil*. Despite the heroism of the sailors and their contempt for death, the Trotskyist Raskolnikov and other traitors succeeded in surrendering the vessels.' In the 1964 edition of Raskolnikov's book this accusation against Trotsky is reduced to an editorial note claiming that he ordered the expedition without consulting the commander-in-chief Vatsetis, who sent an angry telegram to Altvater after the disaster, demanding to know why he had not been informed beforehand.

According to *Five Years of the Red Navy* published in 1922 by the People's Commissariat for Naval Affairs (with a portrait of Trotsky as frontispiece), the commander of the Red Army forces advancing into Estonia had asked for the Navy's assistance in destroying the British ships based at Reval, after they had bombarded Kunda and landed troops in his rear (p.51). *The Trotsky Papers*, Volume I (ed. J.M. Meijer, The

II

Early in the morning of December 25 Altvater, Zarubayev and I travelled in a cold, unheated carriage to Oranienbaum,* where we transferred to an icebreaker bound for Kronstadt. During the journey we talked about the forthcoming operation.

'Be particularly careful of the British light cruisers, which are armed with 6-inch guns and can do 35 knots,' was the advice given to me by Vasily Mikhailovich Altvater. When we reached Kronstadt we found the ships which had been detailed for our expedition fully and ready to set out — except for the destroyer *Avtroil*. Something amiss had been discovered in her engine, and this meant that several more hours would be needed before she was ready for combat. We decided not to put off our departure, and arranged that *Avtroil*, after completing preparations as soon as possible, should quickly catch us up and join our squadron. Altvater and Zarubayev came on board the destroyer *Spartak* (on which I raised my flag) in order to say goodbye to me: final handshakes, advice, good wishes . . .

Kronstadt was completely enclosed by ice. *Spartak's* commander, Pavlinov, skilfully saw to the weighing of our anchor, and at last we quietly got under way. Led by a powerful icebreaker, we cut a path through the dense, rustling masses of ice which thrust at us from every direction, amidst huge floes, breaking up with loud cracks, which banged against the thin, pliant sides of our destroyer. The din made it disagreeable to stay in one's cabin. Accompanied by my assistant for operations, Nikolai Nikolayevich Struisky, I went up on to the bridge. There was a hard frost. Westward, the edge of the

---

Hague, 1964), includes (p.223) a message from Vatsetis to Lenin, dated December 28, demanding an investigation of the affair. He mentions the shortage of coal on one of the ships, *Oleg*, which 'reveals the unpreparedness of the whole operation'.

    The commission of inquiry into the affair reported in February 1919, concluding that it had been a mistake not to see to the adequate fuelling of the ships before they set out, and also that Raskolnikov ought not to have gone ahead alone in *Spartak* when he learnt that *Avtroil* was unable to accompany him.

* Oranienbaum is now called Lomonosov.

icefield showed black, and a strip of dark-grey water gleamed. As we drew closer, this strip widened. At last the gnashing of the ice stopped: we had emerged into the open sea, free from ice-cover. The icebreaker which had escorted us sailed back, puffing thick smoke, towards Red Kronstadt. At the Shepelevsky Light we parted from *Andrei*.

Suddenly *Azard* semaphored that she had not taken on enough fuel.* With a heavy heart I had to send her back to Kronstadt to put this right. Only in the conditions of disorder that prevailed in 1918 could such scandalous errors occur.† Shortly before sunset we encountered the submarine *Pantera*, in the open waters of the Gulf. I ordered her to come alongside. To my question about the results of his reconnaissance the commander of *Pantera* curtly replied that no smoke whatsoever had been observed in Reval harbour.§

Darkness soon fell, and the early December evening set in. Sailing with lights extinguished, we tried not to lose sight of *Oleg*. Suddenly, far off on our starboard bow, a faint light gleamed. We stared at it, and by its regular coming on and going off we recognised the flickering beam of a lighthouse. Soon another lighthouse came into view ahead of us. We almost shouted 'Hurrah!' Lighthouses were shining brightly on the Finnish islands Seiskari and Lavansaari, as though for our convenience. This illumination greatly eased our difficult task of navigation among the islands, sandbanks and submerged rocks of the Gulf of Finland. Late that evening we reached the island of Hogland, rocky and covered with coniferous forest. We sailed all round it and looked into all its inlets, but found

---

* Raskolnikov has not mentioned hitherto how he was intending to use *Azard*. According to *Five Years of the Red Navy* (pp.51-2) she was reconnoitring in Kunda Bay. She returned with a nil report. As she was short of fuel and had something wrong with her engine, it was decided not to involve her in the operation.

† The sentence about 1918 conditions is omitted in the 1936 edition.

§ According to a Soviet source quoted in G. Bennett, *Cowan's War* (1964), *Pantera's* reconnaissance failed because of 'defective compasses, freezing up of periscope and trouble with other equipment, including rudders, trimming tanks, batteries and radio' (p.390).

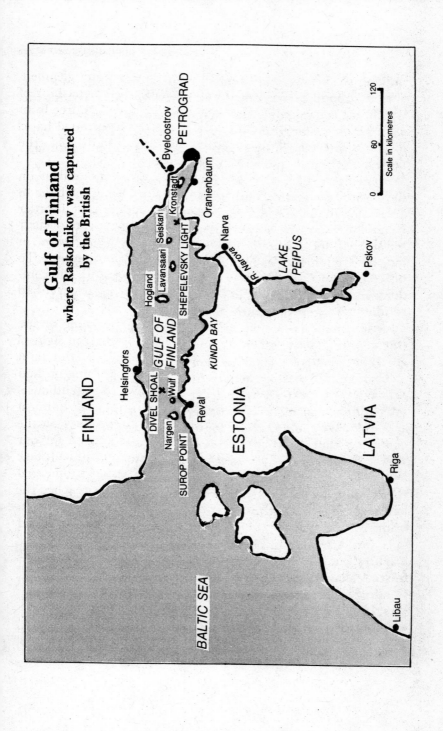

Gulf of Finland
where Raskolnikov was captured by the British

FINLAND

Helsingfors

GULF OF FINLAND

DIVEL SHOAL

Nargen ✕ Wulf

SUROP POINT

Hogland

Lavansaari Seiskari

SHEPELEVSKY LIGHT

✕

Kronstadt

Byeloostrov

PETROGRAD

Oranienbaum

Reval

KUNDA BAY

ESTONIA

Narva

R. Narova

LAKE PEIPUS

Pskov

LATVIA

Riga

BALTIC SEA

Libau

Scale in kilometres

0   60   120

nothing suspicious, and decided to spend the night under its
shelter, dropping anchor on the eastern shore. After posting the
watch, the commanding staff of the destroyer went below. We
sat for a long time, drinking tea and talking, in the cosy wardroom, which was lit by electric lamps and had a big dining-
table in the middle and a black, lacquered piano in one corner.
With me were the modest and reserved commander, Pavlinov,
the cheerful navigator Zybin, who had an inexhaustible fund of
anecdotes, the self-contained gunner Vedernikov, the engineer
Neumann, who was always dissatisfied with something, and
the shrewd, sociable and buoyant Struisky. Our talk 'went on
long after midnight', as bourgeois reporters write.* At last we
broke up and retired to bed in our cabins. After spending a
quiet night in the shelter of Hogland, when dawn came we
assiduously swept the horizon with our binoculars, in every
direction, impatient to spot *Avtroil*, which was late in joining us.
But in vain. The weather continued clear and visibility was
good, but no smoke could be seen anywhere.

Then a coded message arrived from Kronstadt, to tell us that
Avtroil was not yet ready to leave. Her technical hitch had
proved to be considerably more serious than could have been
supposed. We could not wait for her. We had not the slightest
confidence that she would be ready to join us even next day. By
my order the destroyer *Spartak* weighed anchor and set off
alone on our reconnaissance mission, while the cruiser *Oleg*,
commanded by the naval officer Saltanov, remained where she
had spent the night. Struisky, Pavlinov and I went up on to the
bridge.

It was a clear and cloudless winter day. The sun shone
brightly, but its cold, unwarming rays were unable to abate the
frost. A sharp, piercing, icy wind blew, making us who were
standing on the bridge shiver, turn up our collars and rub our
ears. I was wearing a leather jacket lined with fur, but even so I
was chilled to the marrow. The sea was calm, with the absolute

---

* The adjective 'bourgeois' is omitted in the 1936 edition.

stillness that often prevails in these latitudes at the end of December.

III

Not far from Reval smoke appeared on the horizon. We put on speed, hastening towards it, and could soon make out the silhouette of a small merchant vessel.

As we drew nearer we saw that the ship was sailing under the Finnish flag. At that time we had no diplomatic relations with Finland. We made the ship heave to, searched it, and found that it was carrying a cargo of paper destined for Estonia. In view of the crisis in paper supplies at home, this was a valuable prize. A couple of sailors from *Spartak* were transferred to the captured vessel and ordered to take this trophy back to Kronstadt, while we continued our voyage. Soon we had Wulf Island on our beam. If we were to discover how many ships lay in Reval harbour we had to go past Wulf. To ensure the security of this enterprise, however, it was necessary to find out whether there were batteries on the island. In Tsarist times there had been 12-inch batteries on Wulf and Nargen, but in 1918, during the German offensive, our retreating troops had removed these guns. In the circumstances of a hasty withdrawal however, the odd gun might have been left behind, and others might have since been replaced. Also, while they were occupying the island, the Germans might have erected new fortifications. So as to flush out any batteries that could be there, we opened fire on Wulf with our 100-millimetre guns. Our challenge remained unanswered. Evidently there was no artillery on Wulf. This gave us fresh courage, and we continued our bold reconnaissance with enthusiasm. But hardly had we arrived in line with Reval Bay than a column of smoke appeared in the depths of the harbour, then another, then a third, fourth and fifth. Five ominous columns of smoke were moving towards us at lightning speed. Soon we could discern the sharp outlines of warships. As we gazed they grew larger with fantastic speed, the distance between us shrinking rapidly. As soon as we perceived the smoke on the horizon we had made a 180-degree turn and were now going full speed back towards Kronstadt.

It was not long before we were able to make out without difficulty that our pursuers were five British light cruisers, armed with 6-inch guns and capable of a speed exceeding 30 knots. We at once sent a wireless message to *Oleg* describing the situation and calling for support.*

When the gap between us and the enemy had narrowed to the range of gunfire the British were the first to attack. We answered with salvoes from all our guns except the one at the bow, which could not be brought into action because it could not be swug round far enough to fire a shell at the British ships that were overtaking us. This emergency revealed that our destroyer was in a very bad way. Our ranging was so poor that we were unable to see where our own shells were falling. However, the British fired no better, once again confirming their old-established reputation as good navigators but poor gunners.

Seeing that things were in a bad way, that the enemy's considerably superior ships were actually overtaking us, we put both turbines on full speed. The engineers and stokers worked with a will. Although when the destroyer made its test-run after leaving the factory it had achieved a maximum speed of 28 knots, now, under the threat of mortal danger, its mechanism strained hard and produced the unprecedented speed of 32 knots. Our hearts at once felt lighter when we noticed that the distance between us and the enemy vessels was not decreasing.

---

* The Sixth Light Cruiser Squadron — *Cardiff*, *Cassandra*, *Caradoc*, *Ceres* and *Calypso* — commanded by Rear-Admiral Alexander Sinclair, had led the German High Seas Fleet into internment in Scapa Flow in November 1918 and then immediately proceeded to the Baltic accompanied by nine destroyers of the 'V and W' class (one of which, *Wakeful*, is later mentioned by Raskolnikov). *Cassandra* was lost on the way to the Baltic. On December 13 Sinclair shelled the coast near Narva, destroying the only bridge over the river Narova, which was important for the Red Army's communications. He then went off to Latvia with *Cardiff*, *Ceres* and five of his destroyers. The force left at Reval thus consisted of two light cruisers, *Calypso* and *Caradoc*, and four destroyers. On December 24 they landed 200 Estonian shock-troops in Kunda Bay, behind the Red lines.

This meant that we had a chance to get back to Kronstadt from this risky mission of ours, bringing valuable intelligence regarding the strength of the British fleet. Then a stray shell, after flying low over the bridge, splashed into the water near to us. It slightly stunned Comrade Struisky, and the powerful blast crumpled, tore and rendered useless the chart by which we were sailing. This momentarily disorganised our navigation. The helmsman began continually turning his head, not looking ahead so much as checking on where the enemy shells were falling.*

All at once there was a deafening crack. Our destroyer was thrown sharply upward, it vibrated and then suddenly stopped still. We had run on to a submerged reef and all the blades of our screws had been smashed. Behind us a tall spar-buoy stuck up, indicating this dangerous spot.

'Why, this is the notorious Divel Shoal, I know it well. It's shown on every chart. What a stupid thing to happen!' exclaimed Struisky bitterly, in genuine distress.

Seeing the hopeless position our destroyer was in, I sent *Oleg* a message ordering her to get back to Kronstadt.

The British sailors told us later that their admiral,† who was in the leading destroyer, had already given the signal to withdraw: having driven us away from Reval he considered his mission accomplished. When, however, they saw the accident we had suffered, the British ships continued to approach us, not interrupting their gunfire for a single moment. They did not score any hits, even though they were firing at us almost

---

* A partly different account of what happened is given in *Five Years of the Red Navy* (pp.53-54): '*Spartak* was unable to develop full speed because the crew operated the machinery incorrectly and had to stop first one turbine, then the other, so that no more than 23 to 25 knots was achieved. About 1330 hours the blast from *Spartak*'s forward gun, trained too far aft, knocked down the charthouse, scattered and tore the charts, damaged the bridge and concussed the helmsman, so that the ship's position could not be determined. Ten minutes later it was realised from her wash that *Spartak* was in shallow water. Course was altered too late: at about 1340 she stranded on Divel Shoal, losing her screws.' Divel Shoal is now called Kuradimunda.
† Admiral Sinclair was not present. The British force was commanded by Captain B.S. Thesiger (later Admiral Sir Bertram Thesiger) in *Calypso*.

point-blank. Seated on the submerged rocks, our destroyer kept on firing back from the gun at the stern, but was unable to inflict any damage on the enemy. When they perceived what a hopeless position we were in, the British squadron themselves ceased fire, having decided to take the destroyer alive, so to speak. I ordered that our ship be scuttled, but my order was not carried out. Engineer Neumann reported that the sea-cocks would not function. Soon we were surrounded by the British cruisers and they were launching boats to come and board us.

Members of *Spartak*'s crew took me to their quarters and dressed me in a sailor's pea-jacket and quilted coat. Assuring me that they would never betray me, they hastily thrust into my hand the first identity-card they could find belonging to a sailor who had remained ashore. I was transformed into an Estonian from Fellinn district. Since I did not speak Estonian, this was extremely unfortunate, but there was no time to think about that. The destroyer's cook, Comrade Zhukovsky, took charge of my watch.

Before we could look round, British sailors had boarded our destroyer. With the agility of wildcats they rushed into cabins and other living quarters and in the most insolent, cynical and shameless way, proceeded before our very eyes to grab everything they could lay hands on. Then they took us over to their own destroyer. As I sat in the launch I read on their cap-bands the inscription: *Wakeful*. I was struck by their educated-looking faces, their well-cared-for complexions and bright-red cheeks, and at first took these robbers for cadets. However, it turned out that they were ordinary sailors. When we reached *Wakeful*, they put us in the afterhold and gave us ship's biscuits and strong tea. At school I, like everyone else, had learnt languages badly and could only just make out the meaning of spoken English. Nevertheless, I was able to understand quite a lot that I heard. The sailors who brought us our food told us about the British landing at Riga.* In transports of chauvinism, they

---

* Admiral Sinclair in *Cardiff*, landed a small naval force at Riga, then under attack by the Red Army, on December 18. Riga fell to the Red Army on January 3, 1919.

rejoiced at the defeat of Germany: 'Germany is finished. The German fleet is in British ports.'

V

Next morning, *Wakeful*, which had become our floating prison, suddenly upped anchor and set off at speed. Pressing my face to the porthole, I tried in vain to make out where the ship was heading.

'Kunda Bay' was the reply morosely given to my question by the British sailor, armed with a rifle, who guarded us. I knew that Kunda Bay was to the east of Reval. 'In all probability they are taking us to some out-of-the-way spot in order to shoot us there,' was the thought that flashed through my mind.

Then, from above our heads, there was a sudden, deafening sound of gunfire, and after it that soft noise made by the compression of the recoil-absorber which always follows the firing of a gun. There could be no doubt about it: the shot had been fired from the destroyer in which we were held captive. We eagerly rushed to the portholes, but we were so far down in the hold that the field of vision from any of these portholes was small. We could not see anything except the other British destroyers which were sailing near us. The firing ceased as suddenly as it had started. The engine also suddenly stopped. There was a strange silence. The destroyer *Wakeful* had come to a halt. We were taken up to the top deck for exercise. A sad spectacle met our eyes. Right next to us lay the destroyer *Avtroil*, with her topmast awry. She had just been taken by the British, but the red flag still flew over her. The British squadron had come round her from behind and, cutting her off from Kronstadt, had driven her westward, into the open sea. The British commander had ordered us to be let out for exercise at the very moment when *Avtroil* surrendered, so as to wound our revolutionary self-esteem and mock this defeat suffered by the Red Navy. I hastened to cut short our exercise and return to the hold, to the one room in which twenty of the prisoners were

kept. The remaining members of *Spartak*'s crew were being held
in other ships. The commanding staff had been taken ashore.
My companions in misfortune, the sailors of *Spartak*, kept their
spirits up remarkably well, looking with courage into the face of
death. We were all convinced that the British were going to
shoot us.*

VI

On the morning of December 28 we were summoned to go on
deck. Next to the hold there was a tiny compartment containing
the steering-gear. To save me from possible identification the
sailors advised me not to go up but to hide in this place.
However, I was not able to remain there for long. A British sailor
soon found me and took me to the top deck.† Our *Spartak*
men were lined up on the port side of the quarter deck. The
British, together with some White Guards, were making an
intensive search for me. To all their questions the *Spartak* sailors
replied that, before the destroyer left Kronstadt they had
indeed been visited by Raskolnikov, but he had then gone
ashore and had not taken part in the expedition. Not satisfied,
however, with this explanation, the British persisted with their
investigation, evidently possessing definite intelligence that I
was on board *Spartak*.

When I arrived on the top deck I was made to stand to
attention on the left flank of *Spartak*'s crew. In addition to the

---

* According to Captain Thesiger's account of the action, quoted in Bennett, op.cit.,
Spartak had seven officers and 95 men and *Avtroil* had seven officers and 138 men, all
taken prisoner. These prisoners were, with the exception of Raskolnikov and Nynyuk,
handed over to the Estonian Government forces, who kept them on Nargen Island and,
two months later, executed a number of them. The two Soviet destroyers were also
handed over to the Estonian Government: renamed *Vambola* and *Lennuk*, they played an
important part in subsequent operations, being used to land shock-troops in the rear of
the enemy.

† According to Captain Thesiger, quoted in Bennett, op.cit., Raskolnikov was found
'hidden under twelve bags of potatoes'.

British there were some White Guards darting about. They took my identity card from me, and, seeing that, according to this document, I was an Estonian from Fellinn district, a sailor who looked like a boatswain came up to me and began talking in Estonian. I was at once shown up as not knowing that language. To cover myself, I lied, saying that I had long been Russified and had quite forgotten my mother-tongue. At that moment a group of White-Guard officers appeared on the quarterdeck. Among them I at once recognised the tall, lanky figure of a man who had graduated with me from the naval cadet classes — ex-Sub-Lieutenant Fest. By origin Oskar Fest belonged to the Baltic-German nobility. Along with a number of other White-Guard-minded officers, he had remained behind in Reval after the withdrawal of the Red military and naval forces. Fest was the only one of these officers who was wearing civilian clothes. He had on an elegant, brand-new suit, with a dark-blue jacket and carefully-pressed trousers. Despite the frosty day, he was without overcoat or hat. Evidently he had just emerged from the wardroom.

Positioning himself opposite us, on the starboard side, Fest looked slowly along the whole line until he fixed me with his wide-open blue eyes. His long face became even ruddier than usual. He nodded in my direction, named me, and said something to his White-Guard companions. I was at once separated from the rest of the crew, taken to a small cabin, stripped naked, and subjected to a thorough search. Into this cabin suddenly burst a White-Guard wearing a naval officer's uniform. He took a quick look at me and then, choking with joyful excitement, exclaimed loudly to the British sailors who were searching me: 'He is the very man!' Evidently he knew me by sight. When he noticed my sailor's pea-jacket, humble underwear and socks with holes in them, he said, mockingly: 'How you're dressed! And you the Minister of the Navy!' The fact that this White-Guard was allowed free access to me, and his venemous hostility, strengthened still further my conviction that I was certainly going to be shot.

VII

After I had been searched I was taken on deck and made to descend the ladder into a motor-launch. Red-cheeked British sailors, grasping rifles with fixed bayonets, silently escorted me. A mechanic swung a crank-handle vigorously and started the engine, which, after a few splutters, at last shrieked loudly and snorted with the metallic knocking of its pistons. The launch drew slowly and carefully away from the destroyer and then, gaining speed, began to move very fast. I was quite sure that they were taking me to uninhabited and wooded Nargen Island, where it would be convenient for them to shoot me. At such moments religious people begin to say their prayers. As an atheist, my thoughts were that it would not be such a terrible thing to die for my Communist beliefs, for my faith in the righteousness of the cause of the world proletarian revolution.* The only thing that exasperated me was the lengthy time of preparation. Once I was reconciled to the idea that I must inevitably be shot, I wanted the fatal moment to come as quickly as possible. To my amazement, however, the motor-launch made a sharp turn and came round the stern of a light cruiser on whose side I read, in large letters, the name *Calypso*, and then, quickly slackening speed, drew up near the port-side ladder. The admiral's flag flew from the mast: this was the flagship of the British squadron, the light cruiser *Calypso*. The British sailors who were escorting me pointed to the vessel, and called it '*C'lypso*'. Aboard this light cruiser I was put into a tiny cabin in which I could only stand and was barely able to turn round — it was impossible either to sit or to lie down. After I had spent some time in this cell I was led to the admiral's quarters. The admiral sat behind a desk: in a visitor's armchair facing him sat ex-Sub-Lieutenant Fest. Without asking me to sit down, the admiral put the usual questions about my name. I

---

* The word 'world' is omitted from 'world proletarian revolution' in the 1964 edition.

identified myself. Nothing else happened apart from this for-
mality. After quietly discussing something with Fest, the
admiral ordered the sailors to take me away. I was put into a
narrow steam-pipe compartment situated at the ship's side.
There was no porthole. Electric lamps burned there day and
night. It was warm and stuffy from the hot pipes. On the floor,
instead of a bed, lay a broad plank. A sliding grille, like those in
foreign prisons, served as a door. Apparently I was in the place
where sailors were imprisoned. Beside the grille stood a sentry
armed with a rifle. This sailor struck me as a not very agreeable
fellow. Bored with standing on guard, he began to amuse
himself by pointing his rifle at me, closing his left eye, and
pressing on the trigger with the index finger of his right hand. I
knew that a sentry posted to guard me would not dare to shoot
me on the ship itself, so I felt safe. All the same, these jokes were
not to my taste. After sharing with me his joy at the defeat of
Germany and the liquidation of her navy, the sentry again took
aim with his rifle, but this time not at me. 'Lenin,' he barked,
imitating the sound of a shot, and then with a sharp movement
lowered his rifle. I turned away in disgust and withdrew to the
back corner of my floating cell. Then suddenly I heard the
knocking of the engines and from the slight, rhythmic shud-
dering of the hull I realised that the destroyer was weighing
anchor. 'Evidently the British have found it inconvenient to
dispose of me in Reval, a working-class centre, and have
decided to shoot me in some more deserted place,' I
thought.

At noon they brought to me, for lunch, some strong British
tea, without milk or sugar, a few army biscuits and some tinned
food. The tin had been opened, and on the label I read, in
English, 'Rabbit-meat'. Never in my life had I eaten rabbit
and, as always with any unfamiliar dish, I approached this
tinned rabbit-meat with a certain prejudice. To my surprise,
however, rabbit turned out to taste like chicken.

I saw none of the British officers. Not one of them favoured
me with a visit. Only some mechanic, who looked like a re-

engaged fleet-conductor,* came to see me, bringing a sheet of paper, and asked me to write something for him as a souvenir. I readily wrote down some revolutionary verses that I had committed to memory.

Owing to the absence of portholes I could not tell the difference between day and night. I had no watch with me. Judging by the duration of the voyage, however, it must already be evening. I felt like sleeping, and so lay down on the plank.

The light cruiser was going at full speed. An engine was knocking softly and rhythmically somewhere far away. Lulled by the slight trembling of the vessel, I soon fell asleep. When morning came they again brought me tea and biscuits. Then, at last, the engine stopped and the vessel came to a halt. After some time I was taken on deck. I saw that the light cruiser was lying near the shore, in a deserted, wooded locality, thickly covered with snow. In the distance I could make out some single-storey, red-brick, barrack-like buildings. From the deck of the destroyer I was led across a gangplank on to the deck of a passenger-ship that lay alongside. I was ordered to climb down a ladder into the hold of this vessel and lodged in a cabin on the port side. There was a porthole in this cabin. I immediately rushed to it and eagerly pressed my face to the cold glass. But I could see nothing except woods covered with dense snow. Later I heard footsteps: there was a solitary passenger walking about in the adjoining cabin.

VIII

When dusk fell, the ship weighed anchor and left the harbour. Looking through the port-hole, I saw that we were sailing past a long pier, on the end of which was a winking light. To this day I do not know the name of that harbour, but if I were ever to

---

* A 'fleet-conductor' in the Imperial Navy was something like a chief petty-officer — a petty-officer who had passed examinations in technical subjects and took over gunnery or torpedo duties.

find myself there I should recognise it at once, so distinctly are those fleeting impressions engraved in my memory. After passing the pier, the ship turned sharply to port. When I asked where it was heading for my escort did not answer. I began to suspect that I was being taken to Britain. My cabin was separated from my neighbour's only by a thin partition, through which could be heard monotonous, melancholy footsteps and a wheezy cough. My neighbour proved to be a sailor named Nynyuk, the commissar of the destroyer *Avtroil*, a Ukrainian from Volhynia. We spent several days on that ship. It was there that we entered the year 1919. We were not given any books or newspapers. My only diversion was the porthole, at which I spent hours.

Nearly all the time, the ship sailed along a hilly shore which was covered, here and there, with a little snow. From the sun I made out that the ship's course lay westward: the further west we went, the less snow lay on the shore. Although I got no rabbit-meat on this ship, the diet was both better and more plentiful than it had been on the warship. When I knocked at the door, the man in charge of me would come and escort me to the heads. One day, when I woke up, the ship was at anchor. The field of vision available from my cabin down in the hold did not enable me to discover where we had stopped. So I knocked at the door and, accompanied by my escort, went up to the heads: from the porthole there I beheld the panorama of a big city. A forest of factory chimneys, gigantic steam cranes, and, rising above the roofs of innumerable houses, the greenish dome of a big cathedral. From photographs I had seen I recognised the style of this city and guessed that it must be Copenhagen. With a nod my gloomy warder confirmed my supposition.

Soon after this I was summoned on deck, and from there I saw a whole roadstead full of ships both naval and mercantile: not far away lay an entire squadron of destroyers under the multicoloured British flag. By motor-launch I was transferred to the British flagship, the destroyer *Cardiff*, where I was lodged in another stuffy steam-pipe compartment. Comrade Nynyuk was kept strictly separated from me.

The destroyer soon weighed anchor. When I was taken to the top deck for exercise I saw that behind *Cardiff* were sailing, in strict line ahead, several destroyers of the same type.* A whole flotilla was engaged in this cruise. Our voyage across the North Sea was fairly stormy. The destroyer tossed on the waves like the float when an impatient fisherman fitfully tugs on his taut line. Being used to pitching and tossing from my service in the navy, I did not suffer from seasickness. The British sailors rode the storm splendidly and ran about the deck, as it rose beneath them, as gracefully as cats. As we approached the shore of Britain the tossing ceased and the sea grew calm. During all my voyage in *Cardiff* the British sailors showed me amazing friendliness. Saying 'Bolshevik, Bolshevik', and looking round to make sure no officers were about, they thrust into my hands cheese, chocolate and pastries. This was not mere sympathy with a prisoner, but political sympathy with a Bolshevik. The sailors who guarded me did not threaten me with shooting, but benevolently explained that I was to be taken to London.

IX

One day, as I woke up early in the morning, I observed that the destroyer was at anchor. From the porthole of the spacious washroom, to which I was taken every day for my ablutions, I could see an unusually beautiful landscape: high, wooded hills and a huge open-work bridge which traversed a whole bay. 'This is Rosyth,† in Scotland,' the British sailors crowding around me explained. 'Have you ever been here before?' they asked me with friendly interest. I replied that this was

---

* Admiral Sinclair's flagship took refugees from Riga to Copenhagen and there met the other ships of his squadron, from Reval. They all sailed in company to reach Rosyth on January 10.

† Rosyth is on the coast of Fife, near the famous Forth Bridge. During World War I it was used by the Royal Navy as a secondary naval base to Scapa Flow.

absolutely the first time I had visited 'hospitable' Britain. The sailors laughed cheerfully. My sentry gave me notice that that evening I was to be taken to London. And indeed, when darkness fell, I was brought up on deck. There I met Comrade Nynyuk. We were given sailors' caps without ribbons, and yellow woollen capes. A British naval officer ordered that we be handcuffed. The sailor who carried out this order put one pair of handcuffs on the two of us: my left wrist was fettered to Comrade Nynyuk's right. Like this we went down a ladder into a tugboat. We were escorted by a naval officer and two sailors. Complete darkness had now fallen.

Stars shone in the sky. Lights gleamed on both shores of the bay. I did not feel at all cold, although it was already January 9. There was no snow to be seen. The tugboat took us under the lacework bridge with its tall piles and, silently cleaving the calm surface of the water, brought us alongside a deserted barge. A gangplank was laid from the ship to the barge, and we walked across it. This was not easy. The gangplank was very narrow. It would in any case have been hard to keep one's balance on it, and we, being fastened together with handcuffs had to move along it with particular caution, one after another. The handcuffs hindered us frightfully. In danger of slipping, falling into the water and inevitably dragging down one's companion, we at last reached the barge. Beyond this barge, however, instead of the blessed shore, we found a whole series of other barges, lying at anchor and linked together by narrow, swaying gangplanks.

At last we reached the shore, where we were awaited by some policemen in long mackintoshes and tall helmets. We were in a naval port. On the shore lay heaps of coal, and the air was full of fine coal-dust. A large warship lay in dry-dock, looking odd with its keel and armoured side laid bare. We were in Scotland, at Rosyth, one of Britain's major naval bases. The building of this port began as far back as 1909, but it really developed only during the imperialist war. It impressed me as a fully equipped naval base.

X

Without relieving us of our handcuffs, they led us to a small
railway-station where, in a little room belonging to the police,
we had to wait for a train. This arrived after half-an-hour. The
naval officer, youthful, chubby and fair-haired, invited us to get
into a 'soft' carriage.* Our handcuffs attracted attention,
although there were not many passengers either at the station
or in the carriage. We settled into a compartment with seats for
six people. I sat by the window, with Comrade Nynyuk, handcuffed to me, on my left. The officer and the two sailors took
their seats in the same compartment and prudently drew the
curtains over the windows and over the glass panels which gave
on to the corridor. The train slowly started to move. The officer
struck a match , lit his pipe, and gave a light to the sailors. They
began talking together without constraint. The sailors behaved
with great dignity in the presence of the officer. I found myself
making a comparison with the Tsarist Navy. In that navy a
regime of face-slapping prevailed, and ratings did not dare
either to sit or to smoke when an officer was present. In the
British Navy, as in every other, fierce class struggle goes on: on
duty, on a ship of any capitalist navy the ratings are mercilessly
exploited, oppressed and humiliated by the officers. But off
duty, in their free time, British ratings behaved in their dealings
with their officers in a more free-and-easy, independent way
than those of the Tsarist Navy.†

Night soon fell. Our escort, on their soft seats, dropped off
into slumber. I looked out of the window. The train rushed,
rumbling and clanking, past dimly-seen villages and fields that
were neatly ruled in squares, and stopped at stations only
infrequently and briefly. Edinburgh, Scotland's capital, soon

---

* Russian railway-carriages, instead of being categorised as 'first' or 'second class', are
either 'soft' or 'hard'.

† This entire passage contrasting off-duty relations between officers and other ranks in
the British and Russian navies is omitted in both the 1936 and 1964 editions.

flew by. As we travelled southward the scenery underwent a marked change. The Scottish hills gradually gave place to the plains of England. I could not sleep in my uncomfortable situation. Suddenly I noticed that the handcuffs, which fitted closely the big-boned wrist of Comrade Nynyuk, were too big for me. When I tried to pull my hand out of the iron bracelet, I did so with ease. I glanced at the escort: they were sweetly and serenely asleep. I at once thought of escaping. This would have been all the easier in that the outside door was in the compartment itself, and all I should have to do, sitting as I was by the window, was to turn the door-handle and jump out. The temptation was great. But the train was hurtling along at a tremendous speed, unknown in Russia. So I decided to get away when we stopped. I even imagined how, with the help of British workers, I might make my way over to the Continent and from there to Soviet Russia.

I was used to being deprived of freedom. In 1912 I had been in the pre-trial detention centre and in the German prison at Insterburg, and in 1917 I had been in the Kresty prison. But after my lively revolutionary activity in 1917 and 1918 I found it particularly hard not to be at liberty. I was tormented with desire to work for the good of the young Soviet republic, and yet, here I was, in captivity. Unfortunately, the engine-driver braked the train only at the last moment, just as we were entering the station. The sudden halt woke up our escort. They shook their heads and with astonishment gazed at me out of their sleepy eyes.

So I did not manage to escape. Early in the morning one of the sailors bought a newspaper at an intermediate station. While the officer was out of the compartment the sailor showed me the paper and, laughing, put his finger on the place where some report appeared. I read it, and also could not refrain from laughter. The report began with the triumphant words: 'We have captured the First Lord of the Bolshevist Admiralty.' The combination of such contradictory concepts as 'Lord' and 'Bolshevism' was unexpected and tasteless. This was how a British

bourgeois newspaper conveyed, in language understandable
by its readers, my position as a member of the Revolutionary
War Council of the Republic.

XI

We reached London in the damp and foggy morning of January
10, 1919.*

There was a thin, brisk drizzle falling. In a covered car which
was waiting for us at the station our naval guard took us to the
Admiralty. We were both made to wait in a corridor, still
wearing handcuffs. Admiralty officials, typists and secretaries
hurried past us. While seeming to be busy with their work they
nevertheless kept looking curiously at us. They were evidently
interested to see real live Bolsheviks, brought straight from
Soviet Russia. Soon, we were relieved of our handcuffs and led,
first of all, into a big room of the government-office type in
which several men in naval officers' uniform were seated round
a table. At the head of the table sat a stout, clean-shaven,
red-cheeked admiral of about 50. Beside him was a man with
fair hair smoothed down on either side of a parting, a fair
moustache, but no beard, and wearing the uniform of a British
naval officer. The admiral put questions to me in English, and
the fair-haired man translated them into such impeccable Russian that at first I even took him for a Russian White Guard.
However, certain turns of phrase later showed me that he must
be a genuine Englishman. The first question put to me by the
admiral caused me much surprise: 'What can you tell us about
the murder of Captain Cromie?'

I replied that I could tell them absolutely nothing. I remem-
bered that our newspapers had reported the killing of a certain
Lieutenant Cromie in the building of the British Embassy in
Petrograd when, obstructing the entry of a detachment sent to

---

* Bruce Lockhart records in his *Diaries*, Vol.I (1973) that on this day he was 'sent for
by Foreign Office to discuss question of Raskolnikov's capture by our fleet near Reval'
(p.52).

Execution of a Bolshevik on board a British ship

carry out a search, he had been the first to open fire from his revolver on the Soviet militia. I had had nothing at all to do with this event.

'All the same, this was the work of your hands,' said the admiral, mistrustfully. 'Of course, I am not saying that you personally took part in the murder. But there can be no doubt that it was the doing of Uritsky and company.'

At that moment this thought flashed through my mind: was, perhaps, the killing of Comrade Uritsky by Kanegisser organised by the British as revenge for the killing of Cromie?* I rejected with indignation the suggestion that the death of Lieutenant Cromie had been premeditated by any representative of the Soviet power.

'This was a fatal accident such as can happen in any armed clash — a clash which, in this instance, as far as I am aware, was initiated by Lieutenant Cromie himself,' I said.

The British officers then asked me about the circumstances of my capture. Finally, they asked me how many destroyers and how many sailors had been transferred from the Baltic to the Caspian? I said that this was a military secret, and refused to answer. In fact, all that business had been managed by me and I knew exactly how many ships and sailors had been sent to the Caspian through the Mariinskaya system† and down the river Volga. My refusal to answer irritated the British officers somewhat. They raised their voices, but, when convinced that it was useless to question me further, they gave up.

After Comrade Nynyuk had been interrogated, we were manacled once more and led out into the street.

XII

At the entrance to the Admiralty stood an open motor-car

---

* Actually, Uritsky was killed on August 30, and the Cheka's raid on the British Embassy, in which Cromie met his death, took place on the following day, August 31.

† The Mariinskaya system was the series of canals which linked the port of Petrograd with the river Volga.

around which, as we appeared, there quickly gathered a crowd of passers-by and small boys, who stared at us with amazement, as though we were polar bears. Accompanied by the fair-haired officer and some armed sailors we were taken in this car to Scotland Yard, the headquarters of Britain's political police.

Scotland Yard occupies a very large, many-storeyed building in the best part of London.* Waiting to see us there was the head of the British political police, Sir Basil Thomson.†

A tall, lean, elegantly-dressed old man, young-seeming for his age, with a carefully-clipped moustache, Basil Thomson received me in his office. At another table, by the wall, sat a shorthand-writer. Thomson did not ask me to sit down. Through the interpreter he asked me about the circumstances of my capture. Then he expressed interest in my life-story. This was no secret, so I related it. The shorthand-writer industriously recorded my statements.

'So, then, you're a Bolshevik?' Thomson asked, with unconcealed surprise and curiosity.

'Yes,' I replied, 'I'm a Bolshevik.'

They took me into an adjoining room. After a few minutes the fair-haired officer who had acted as my interpreter at the Admiralty and at Scotland Yard came out of Thomson's office. He told me that I was to be held as a hostage for the safety of British personnel who were in Bolshevik hands. I was to answer for their well-being, all and severally. 'Whatever fate befalls them, that fate will be yours,' said the fair-haired naval officer, significantly. He added that the British Government was ready to exchange me for a British naval officer, related to Sir Edward Grey, and three sailors who had been taken prisoner by us while making a reconnaissance somewhere in the forest on the northern front, not far from Archangel. According to the

---

* At this time 'Scotland Yard' occupied a building on Victoria Embankment, near Westminster Bridge.

† Thomson (1861-1939) was Director of Intelligence at Scotland Yard in 1919-1921. When Raskolnikov met him he was not yet 'Sir Basil'.

information the British possessed, they were in Moscow, in Butyrski Prison. It was proposed that I should send a telegram to this effect to the Council of People's Commissars. I asked for a piece of paper and scribbled a telegram. To my text the British added a note that the Soviet Government's reply should be addressed to London, to an institution entitled the 'Peace Parliament'. The fair-haired officer undertook to send off this telegram forthwith, by wireless.* I was taken into another room and asked to wait. This was the office of some official of the political police. In the corner a fire burned in a big grate, in front of which a bald-headed police official was warming himself and drinking strong tea, accompanied by white bread-rolls.

They sat me down at a table and gave me, too, some tea and rolls. This came at the right moment, as I had had nothing to eat since early morning.

The British Government pays well for the services of its police agents. All these detectives are dressed in elegant jackets. Their trousers have knife-edge creases. At night they do not hang their trousers up but place them on a chair beside the bed, in a wooden press consisting of two parallel oaken planks. The British sleuths do their best to cultivate the outward appearance of 'gentlemen'.†

When I had drunk my tea I was taken out into the corridor. At that moment Sir Basil Thomson, wearing a top-hat glossy as a mirror, passed me, walking with the slow gait of a tired old dodderer, and solemnly proceeded out into the street. After a short interval Comrade Nynyuk joined me, and we were taken outside, to where a car awaited us. Two detectives of incredible

---

* The text of Raskolnikov's telegram is in the British Foreign Office archives (FO 371/3938). The telegram was addressed to Trotsky and said that the British authorities 'state they are willing to release me in return for all British now arrested in Russia', together with a Belgian merchant navy captain named Schoonjans (who eventually got out under a separate arrangement). 'Peace Parliament' was the telegraphic address to be used for correspondence with the Foreign Office on prisoner exchange with Soviet Russia.

† The entire passage about the clothing of members of the CID is omitted in the 1964 edition.

stoutness got into the car with some difficulty; there was hardly
room for the four of us in that little closed car. The detectives
both wore silky-smooth bowler-hats. The car started, crossed
the bridge over the Thames, and hurtled rapidly down a long,
broad street. Soon it turned right, into a narrow side-street, and
came to a stop outside the massive gates of a prison.

Rattling heavy keys, an ungracious guard gloomily opened
the gates and led us into the prison reception-office. The detectives handed us over, like packets of goods, against a receipt
made out by the man in charge, and then, raising their bowlers,
took leave of us. As in every prison in the world, we were
subjected to a short questionnaire: surname, forenames,
occupation, religion. When it came to the last of these points,
the official who was filling in the form found himself stymied.
He could not make out which church I belonged to. In reply to
his question: 'Are you Catholic or Protestant?' I answered
firmly, 'Neither, I'm an atheist.' 'A Catholic?' he asked me
again, obviously not understanding what I had said. 'Atheist,'
I replied, patiently. 'Greek Church?' 'No, atheist.' 'So, you're a
Protestant?' 'I tell you I'm an atheist,' I insisted. In the end he
wrote me down, all the same, as a member of the Greek Church,
on the grounds that, before the revolution the Orthodox
Church had been the state religion in Russia. Then I was taken
to the bathroom, where, on either side of a corridor, behind thin
partitions, there were white baths. I eagerly washed myself,
and changed into government-issue underwear. I was allowed
not to wear prison clothes but to keep my own, that is, the
sailor's pea-jacket which I had worn ever since I was given a
change of clothes on *Spartak*. As upper garment I had a sailor's
quilted double-breasted coat, and the yellow cape, with a hood,
which had been given me on *Cardiff* before I set out for London.
On my head I wore a British sailor's cap, shaped like a pancake
and without ribbons. From the bath I was led to a one-man cell.
As I passed through the inner corridors of the prison I realised
with what dreary uniformity all the world's prisons resemble
each other.

Brixton Prison reminded me most of the Kresty Prison in Petrograd. The same corridors, the same stairways, even the same crosswise arrangement of the blocks. My cell was on the ground floor and its barred window looked out on the prison yard, where prisoners were taking exercise, dressed in grey suits and narrow, oblong caps, also grey. I was in the block called D Hall — Section One, cell number three. Comrade Nynyuk was lodged in the adjoining cell. The warder — called in British prisons a 'prison officer' — slammed the heavy door behind me, turned the key twice in the lock, and slowly walked away. I was left on my own. For lack of anything else to do I measured the size of my cell. How dreary! Exactly the same amount of floor-space as in Russian prisons: five paces one way and three paces the other. Exactly the same furniture: a narrow bed, fastened to the wall, an iron table and a little stool. On a shelf in one corner lay a Bible, and on the floor, instead of a close-stool, there was a chamber-pot.

On the door of my cell was a board inscribed: 'Prisoner-of-war.'

XIII

Day followed day. Comrade Nynyuk and I were subjected to a strict regime of solitary confinement. Every morning, after the bell had rung to awaken the prisoners, a warder, rattling a bunch of huge keys, opened the door of my cell and loudly announced: 'Applications'.* Beside him at the door stood another prison official, who always carried a slate, on which he would write in chalk the prisoners' applications. Through this official one could send for the doctor, order food or newspapers, arrange for a better meal to be served, in return for special payment, ask for paper and envelopes in order to write letters, or make some complaint. After this round had been completed, the warder on duty would open the cell again, shouting: 'Bring out slops.'† This meant that we had to bring out the chamber-

---

* Raskolnikov writes, in English: 'The application'.
† Raskolnikov writes, in English: 'Bring a slops'.

pot which substituted for the usual Russian close-stool. We had
to wash in the lavatory, as there was no water laid on in the
cells. After that, a bucket of hot water was brought, together
with a rag, a brush and some wax. I had to wash the floor with
hot water and then polish it with wax. The wooden top of the
table had to be scrubbed with the brush provided. After this
cleaning had been accomplished we were given our morning
tea, without sugar, along with a small white roll and a tiny piece
of margarine. Butter and sugar, like eggs, were rationed at that
time, and there was not enough for us prisoners. These food-
stuffs could not be had even for money. The warder's next visit
was accompanied by the cry: 'Exercise.' At first I did not
understand what this meant. With my inadequate knowledge
of English I took this word to mean exercise in the sense of the
practising of some skill. What sort of exercise could this be, I
wondered, as I stood in the midst of my cell, not knowing what
to do. 'Exercise,' repeated the elderly, whiskered warder, and
beckoned me to come out. By empirical experience I learnt that
the English word 'exercise' has another meaning — taking a
walk. We walked in a circle, in the prison yard, which was
surrounded by a high brick wall. This was the only place where
I could meet Comrade Nynyuk. I was sometimes able, evading
the warders' vigilance, to exchange a few words with him.
Unfortunately, our exercise did not last long — between 15
minutes and half an hour. After that we were settled back into
our cells. At midday lunch was brought round: this consisted
mainly of potatoes. Unlike what happened in Russian prisons,
we were not given soup every day. On Sundays the potatoes
were replaced by a special dish, a small piece of bright-red
corned beef. Finally, when evening came, we had our supper: a
mug of cocoa, made with water and without sugar, together
with a roll. Soon after supper the prisoners had to go to bed.

On one of my first days in prison I asked for an envelope and
paper and wrote a letter to Comrade M. M. Litvinov, informing
him, as our representative, of my involuntary presence in London and detention in Brixton Prison. I told him that I needed

F.F. Raskolnikov

money and Russian books, and asked him to pay me a visit. After a few days the letter was returned to me with a brief explanation that Litvinov had already been deported from Britain.

On another occasion I sent a letter to my mother but this was quickly returned to me, unsealed, with the inscription: 'opened by censor', and, on the other side the significant words, impressed by a rubber stamp: 'communication suspended'.

Finally, when I wanted to send a telegram, I was first refused this on the excuse that I should soon be released, and then told that I could not do it because there was no telegraphic communication with Russia.

XIV

In the prison there was a library, which at once became my chief helpmate in whiling away my involuntary leisure.

This library was in the charge of the prison schoolmaster, who combined his teaching duties with responsibility for the prison library. The grey face of this elderly person was always edged, as though with fur, with the bristles of an unshaven beard. The dove-coloured nose on his grey face revealed his morbid addiction to alcohol. The librarian did not speak French so much as love to show off his knowledge of a foreign language. All the same, this did facilitate my dealings with him. The prison library consisted mainly of the works of classical English authors — Shakespeare, Dickens, Thackeray — together with illustrated journals of the lighter sort, such as the *Strand Magazine*, with the writings of Conan Doyle and Phillips Oppenheim. The section devoted to theological and religious literature was well stocked. There was also a small number of French books. In Russian there were only Tolstoy's *The Cossacks* and *Anna Karenina*. The library was small and its selection of books a random one. From the first days of my imprisonment I set myself to study English. It turned out that even the Bible could come in useful for this purpose. From lack of anything

else to do I started to peruse it and, as I knew the corresponding
Russian text, I could guess at the meaning of certain words and
try to memorise them. There was no English-Russian dictionary in the library. I therefore took out the English-French
dictionary and, making use of my comparatively better knowledge of French, gradually began, with the aid of this dictionary, to read English books.

XV

One day at the beginning of February I was summoned to the
reception office, where a lanky detective was waiting for me. He
led me out into the street, clambered with me on to the top of a
huge double-decker bus, and took me to the centre of London.

The usual London rain was falling. The streets through
which we passed were full of feverish activity. There came into
my mind the opening words of Valery Bryusov's poem *The Pale
Horse*:

> The street was like a storm. Crowds went by
> As though chased by an inescapable fate.
> Buses, cabs, motor-cars, all rushed along.
> The flood of human beings was tireless and furious.*

Waiting for me in one of the rooms in the Admiralty was the
naval officer who had acted as interpreter when I was interrogated there and at Scotland Yard. Seated beside him at a
table was another naval officer, stout, with grey-streaked dark
hair, a thick moustache and a pointed, neatly-trimmed beard.
He introduced himself as Britain's former naval representative
at the headquarters of the Black Sea Fleet. He had spent the
imperialist war and the first months of the revolution at Sebastopol. This time, the British seamen asked me to sit down at
their table and subjected me to a cross-examination regarding the theoretical foundations of Communism. They were

---

* This poem by Valery Bryusov (1873-1924) was written in 1904. It describes a sudden
death due to a street accident.

particularly interested in our economic and political conceptions. Later, they gave me the depressing news of the deaths of Karl Liebknecht and Rosa Luxemburg, and also of the landing of the Allied expeditionary force at Odessa.* I had known nothing of any of this because, having no British money, I could not buy newspapers. The British seamen offered to change into British money the six Tsarist ten-rouble notes which had been taken off me when I entered prison. In addition to these I also had a few square forty-rouble and twenty-rouble 'Kerensky' notes. These, however, the British officers smilingly declined to change. Anyway, I now had nearly three pounds sterling. First and foremost, I hastened to provide myself with underclothes. The next time the warder came round for 'applications' I put myself down for two flannel shirts, two pairs of pants and two pairs of woollen socks. These purchases cost me dear, nearly two pounds sterling, absorbing a substantial proportion of my money. In addition, I bought myself four small, cheap dictionaries, bound in red calico, published by Garnier Frères:† English-Russian, Russian-English, French-Russian and Russian-French. After that, I was left with less than a pound. With this money I began buying newspapers every day. Thereafter, my knowledge of English increased so fast that, within a month, I was able to read a newspaper without using a dictionary. My principal reading consisted of *The Times* and the *Daily News*. I bought the reactionary *Times* for the sake of its extensive coverage, easily putting up with its publication of the most incomprehensible concoctions about Soviet Russia. The Liberal *Daily News* was the most left-wing paper I was allowed to read. I tried several times without success to order the *Manchester Guardian*:§ the warders always gave me the

---

* Allied troops had landed at Odessa on December 18 1918. Liebknecht and Luxemburg had been murdered on January 15 1919.

†Garnier Frères were an old-established Paris publishing house.

§ The *Manchester Guardian* (now the *Guardian*), although printed in Manchester, was available at this time at main railway stations and many newsagents in London. Its publication in 1918 of the pro-Bolshevik despatches by Morgan Philips Price had doubtless caused the authorities to put it on their black list.

ridiculous excuse that this paper was published not in London but in Manchester.

At this time all the British newspapers were getting their information about Soviet Russia through their correspondents in Riga and Helsingfors, whose principal source was the White-Guard émigrés. Consequently, the most fantastic calumnies filled the pages of the British bourgeois press. Every day I came upon some astounding piece of news. Thus, I suddenly learnt that Chinese were selling human flesh in the streets of Moscow, and then that the death-rate in Russia had risen so high that there was a shortage of wood for coffins. The Red Army was always depicted as a rabble of Chinese and Letts. I carefully cut out all the articles and reports concerning Soviet Russia: they made a very strong-smelling bouquet. Alas, when I returned to Russia, this rich collection was taken from me by the British, on the basis of the war-time law known from its initials as 'Dora',* which prohibited the export of printed matter.

Through reading the newspapers I was able, even though in prison, to keep well in touch with international affairs, and in particular with the progress of the peace talks at Versailles which had then just begun.

The Russian question was frequently raised and discussed in Parliament. The advocates of resolute intervention against Soviet Russia openly voiced their dissatisfaction with Lloyd George's half-hearted policy. They urged that Soviet power be overthrown by despatching a large army to Russia. But Lloyd George, who took account of the war-weary mood of the peasant masses [sic] and was afraid of the workers, among whom sympathy with the land of the Soviets was growing day by day, dominated the policy of his cabinet. I remember that one day, parrying the blows of the Conservatives, he said,

* The Defence of the Realm Act ('DORA'), passed in 1914, gave the British Government extensive powers for the duration of the war.

referring to the example of Napoleon: 'Russia is a country it is easy to get into but hard to get out of.'*

The Government was frequently asked: 'What is happening to the British officers who are held by the Bolsheviks?' One day the deputy-minister for foreign affairs, Amery, said in answer to this question that the British Government was negotiating with the Soviet Government, through the Danish Red Cross, about an exchange of these officers for Russian Bolsheviks held in Britain.† I realised that this statement must refer to me, amongst others, and looked forward impatiently to the end of the negotiations.

From these British newspapers I learnt of the death of Comrade Sverdlov, of the arrest of Comrade Radek in Germany, and of the detention in France of Comrade Manuilsky.§

One day I read in the papers about the proposal made to us and to the White Guards by the 'Allies' for a conference to be held at Prinkipo, in the Princes' Islands. Soon afterward I learnt that the Soviet Government had agreed to this proposal, but that the conference had not taken place, because Denikin and Kolchak had refused to attend.

I had dreamt of going to that conference, so as thereby to get out of prison. As I learnt subsequently my name had indeed been put forward as one of the Soviet delegates.

After newspapers I started on books. One of the first English books I read was Hilaire Belloc's *The French Revolution*.**

---

* Lloyd George's remark concerning Russia ('It is a country which it is easy to get into but very difficult to get out of') was made on April 16 1919.

† This statement was made, on March 27 1919, by Cecil Harmsworth, who was Under-Secretary for the Colonies.

§ Radek attended the founding congress of the Communist Party of Germany at the end of December 1918. He was arrested on February 15, 1919. Manuilsky was sent to France in January 1919, as a member of a Red Cross delegation, to arrange repatriation of Russian soldiers still in France. When they landed at Dunkirk they were arrested and interned at Malo-les-Bains, a suburb of that town.

** Hilaire Belloc's short book on the French Revolution was published in 1911 in the popular series The Home University Library.

XVI

Lying hypocrisy reigns in all Britain's prisons. Along with a cheap tin plate and an earthenware mug, the inventory of every cell includes a Bible and a Prayer book. Three mornings a week the prisoners attend religious services. 'Chapel, chapel,' shouts the prison officer, and he leads the prisoners into the corridor by which, in single file, they make their way to the prison chapel. There they are seated on long, narrow benches. Some of them make a rattling noise with every movement during the service, from the heavy manacles fettering their hands and feet.

I too went to chapel several times, mainly so as to listen to the organ. The small, unprepossessing organist, wearing a black gown, approached with rapid steps, adjusting his spectacles in an embarrassed way, and as though furtively, the high sonorous organ which stood by the left-hand wall. The face and the entire miserable figure of this organist bore the marks of the burdens of a large family and tormenting worry about a crust of dry bread. He played the organ remarkably well. Despite the fact that the hymns were quite alien to me, into the monotony of prison life even this dreary music brought a certain diversion.

The plump Anglican clergyman was the complete opposite of the organist. Wearing silver-rimmed spectacles, with an impressive head of grey hair, carefully parted, and fat cheeks that shone with good living, this man, dressed in a white cassock like a loose overall, read the prayers unhurriedly, in a sing-song voice and the prisoners chorused the responses. After the liturgy, this heavy, clumsy man climbed up, awkward as a hippopotamus emerging from the water, into the pulpit and, adjusting his long, wide, inconvenient sleeves, in which his white, puffy hands, carefully tended since childhood, were hopelessly lost, he began desperately and frightfully denouncing the Russian Bolsheviks. This struck me as funny, and I was unable to repress a smile.

XVII

The London winter was mild. Fog, rain, soft snow which soon melted on the ground. They do not have hard frosts there. When large flakes of damp snow began to fall, the fat, red-faced warders, panting from obesity and clanking their bunches of keys, who opened the door into the yard for me would rub their hands with cold and exclaim with horror: 'Siberia, Siberia!' I laughed and shook my head. Poor fellows, they had no notion of the real cold of our Siberia, with which no London winter can be compared. They do not heat the prisons in London, or else heat them very poorly. At all events, it was cold in my cell. I had to wear my pea-jacket all the time. My cell was at ground level, and damp came up through the stone floor. During that winter there was a severe epidemic of Spanish influenza in Britain. Every day the newspapers reported the deaths of entire families from this illness. I went down with a cold, but fortunately, the flu epidemic spared Brixton Prison, and I got away with nothing worse than a cold. Nevertheless, I put in for a visit by the doctor. The British doctor sounded my chest, gave me some medicine and, when he learnt that I found the prison food inadequate, prescribed a reinforced diet. This meant that every day I now received, along with my morning tea, some porridge. I had little money left and so had to be satisfied with the prison diet. Just as in the Tsarist prisons, in Brixton Prison one could get a better meal if one paid specially for it. Such a meal cost one shilling. One day I ordered it just to see what it was like. It proved to be very pleasant, consisting of soup and English roast beef with greens. In bourgeois society class differences exist everywhere, and the well-to-do can live not badly even in a British prison.

XVIII

When my mastery of English had improved, I decided to pass it on to my comrade Nynyuk. Hastening my pace as we walked in a circle during exercises I would catch up with him and, when the warder's attention was elsewhere, quickly say to him:

'*Koshka* — cat, *ryba* — fish.' Running round at a fast rate so as to
warm myself up, I would approach Comrade Nynyuk again
and whisper: '*Koshka* — cat, *ryba* — fish. Repeat that!' '*Koshka* —
fish, *ryba* — cat,' he would reply, always getting it the wrong
way round. Nothing came of these English lessons. He had
much greater success in grasping the political news which I
managed to pass on to him during exercise.

When other prisoners, mostly criminals, were brought out
for exercise, we, being 'dangerous Bolsheviks', were kept strictly
apart from them and made to walk to and fro in a straight line at
a tangent to the circle. One day there was sent out for exercise
with us a short, hunchbacked man without a cap on his shock of
thick hair. When we encountered each other I begn to talk with
him. I managed to discover that his name was Kerran and that
he was a member of the British Socialist Party and had been in
prison four years already, for agitating against the war. When
he learnt that we were Russian Bolsheviks he showed us
marked friendliness. Once, when the prison officer was not
looking, as Kerran came level with me during our exercise, he
dropped a package on the ground. I hastened to pick it up. It
consisted of several issues of the left-wing workers' journals *The
Call* and *The Herald*. From them I learnt that the British workers' leader John Maclean had been released from prison and
triumphantly welcomed by the workers. As I read these journals I appreciated what a vigorous campaign was being waged
against intervention by the British working class under the
leadership of their Communists. A meeting attended by many
thousands had been held in London's huge Albert Hall, under
the slogan: 'Hands off Russia!'* The British workers were not
only protesting but actively fighting against aid to the White
Guards, against intervention by British troops. Lloyd George
was compelled to take account of this feeling among the working class in Britain.

---

* The Albert Hall meeting on February 8 1919 initiated the 'Hands off Russia'
movement of 1919-1920.

Scottish workers' leader John Maclean

XIX

The population of the prison was large and variegated. The overwhelming majority of its inmates were criminal prisoners. Once, during exercise, I made the acquaintance of a certain Russian, born in Canada, who had served with the Canadian forces in the war and was now in prison for some offence. He had become quite 'anglicised'. He spoke his Russian mother-tongue very poorly, with a strong accent, but could talk and write fluently in English.

As in every prison, the population of Brixton Prison fluctuated. Sometimes we were joined by other 'politicals'. At that time they were carrying out mass arrests of Russians suspected of Bolshevism. These persons were deported from Britain as undesirable aliens. Once, during exercise, Kerran, whose cell was in a different block, told me that a large number of Russians suspected of Bolshevist sympathies had been brought to the prison. Soon afterward there arrived in our D Hall one of these suspects, a hairdresser named Morgenstern. He was deported to Russia, and later on, in 1921, I came across him again, in Krasnodar.*

The winter ended and spring came. Some feeble grass came up in the yard, but I still lay in prison, as though forgotten. I had got pretty fed up with being shut in. Spring urged me towards freedom, greenery, the open air.

Sometimes during exercise the idea of escape entered my head, but I had to reject it at once. The high brick walls and the alert watchfulness of the warders presented insurmountable obstacles. I remembered that the Irish bourgeois revolutionary De Valera escaped from a British prison. But he had been freed by the Sinn Fein organisation.† I had no contacts in Britain.

Then, one day at the beginning of May, I was told to collect

---

* The passage about Morgenstern does not appear in the 1964 edition.

† Eamonn de Valera was imprisoned in 1916 for his part in the Easter Rebellion, but released in the following year. Arrested again in 1918, he was put into Lincoln Prison, but escaped in February 1919.

up all my belongings and was taken by car to Scotland Yard. Comrade Nynyuk went with me. At Scotland Yard we were informed that, as the regime under which the British officers were kept in Moscow had been mitigated, and they were being allowed comparative freedom, we too were to be transferred to a hotel, under surveillance by the police and on condition that we did not leave London. After that, accompanied by a detective, we were taken to the Mills Hotel in Gower Street,* not far from the British Museum. We were assigned a small, modestly furnished room on the first floor. Here we spent twelve days in freedom. At first we had no money. After a few days, however, someone from Scotland Yard called on me to say that the Danish Embassy had received some money from Moscow that was meant for me.† He accompanied me on a journey by the underground railway, with some complicated changes, which brought us to the remote, aristocratic quarter of London where the Danish Embassy was situated.§

Through a reception-room neat as a box of sweets I was led into the austere and businesslike office of the Minister. A tall, grey-haired man handed me fifty pounds sterling, sent to me by the People's Commissariat for Foreign Affairs through the good offices of the Danish Red Cross Mission, who were apparently the only foreign representatives left in Moscow. The officious sleuth accompanied me back to my residence. Then Comrade Nynyuk and I went to an off-the-peg clothing shop in Oxford Street and changed into decent suits. At a hat shop we bought ourselves soft felt hats, to replace the sailors' caps without

---

* In 1919 a Mrs Florence Mills kept a hotel which occupied eight houses in Gower Street, Bloomsbury, near University College.

† Correspondence in FO 371/3939 and 3940 includes a letter from Raskolnikov to Larissa Reissner, despatched at the beginning of April, urging her to arrange his repatriation as soon as possible, and a telegram from her saying: 'Your exchange is nearly arranged . . . The Danish Embassy in London will give you necessary funds for linen and clothing, the expense of which we shall meet in Moscow.' The British Red Cross Society's representative in Moscow informed the Foreign Office that 'Raskolnikov's wife is a personage of considerable importance in the Soviet Government.'

§ In 1919 the Danish Minister's offices were in Pont Street, near Knightsbridge.

ribbons that we had been given on *Cardiff*. From semi-ragamuffins who attracted attention in the fashionable streets of London we were transformed into properly-dressed people.

In the course of these twelve days I succeeded in acquainting myself with London and its places of note. First of all I visited the British Museum, which, with its rich archaeological and artistic collections, made a big impression on me. Then I went to the Zoo. At Covent Garden Theatre I heard the opera *Tosca*, in which some first-class Italian singers performed.*

On one of these days of freedom I visited the Central Committee of the British Socialist Party. This was huddled in dark and dirty little rooms somewhere in Drury Lane.† They received me politely and correctly, but without any marks of cordial hospitality.

I went again to the Admiralty, to find out when, at last, I was to be returned to Soviet Russia, where I strongly wished to be, so as once more to take part in the civil war. An officer in a khaki service-jacket told me that the negotiations regarding the time and place of the exchange had already been completed, and I should probably be sent back to Russia, through Finland, in the next day or so.

One day a young man in a civilian overcoat called on us and told us to get ready to leave. He explained that he was to accompany us to Rosyth. We soon gathered up our possessions and carried them out into the street. We were taken in a car to Scotland Yard, where Sir Basil Thomson received us once again. He explained that we were to be sent to Russia through Finland because the exchange with the British officers would be effected on the Finnish-Soviet frontier. In the same car and accompanied by the same young policeman we were then taken to the railway station. There, people were seeing off some

---

* The Royal Opera House reopened after the war on May 12 1919, and a performance of *Tosca* was given on May 16.

† The headquarters of the British Socialist Party was in 1919 in Maiden Lane, between Covent Garden and the Strand. No doubt Raskolnikov, coming from Gower Street, approached it via Drury Lane.

British volunteers who were going to Murmansk and Archangel to help the Russian White Guards. Facing us in our compartment of the train sat a long-faced British officer. In our conversation with him it emerged that he was on his way to fight against us as a volunteer. At Leeds [*sic*]* he was going to change on to a steamship. Dusk gradually descended. Evening came on. It grew cold in the compartment. Comrade Nynyuk shivered. The British officer removed his overcoat and offered it to my comrade, although he knew quite well that we were Bolsheviks. What was this? The act of a gentleman, or a pose by a class enemy playing at magnanimity? Most probably the latter: but, in any case, it was a handsome gesture.†

XXI

We arrived at Rosyth early in the morning. The policeman led us to the steamer *Greenwich* and, after handing us over to the naval authorities, left at once. On *Greenwich* we were placed in the care of a round-faced non-commissioned officer of the Marines, who perform the role of gendarmes on ships of the British navy. *Greenwich*, a fairly large armed vessel which served as a submarine tender, was going to Copenhagen. Hardly had we moved off when a grey-moustached mechanic, puffing at his pipe, loquaciously related to me the story of how the German sailors had scuttled the German fleet interned at Scapa Flow.§

The green and hilly shores of Scotland were soon hidden below the horizon and the steamer emerged into the open sea. I asked our round-faced NCO whether he knew any foreign

---

* 'Leeds' may be a mis-hearing of 'Leith'.

† The report, dated May 20 1919, by the CID officer who escorted Raskolnikov to Inverkeithing, the railway station for Rosyth, which is in FO 371/3941, says: 'Prior to embarking, Raskolnikov expressed his gratitude for the treatment received by himself and his companion whilst in the hands of the British authorities, and requested me to convey his thanks to Mr Thomson for the courtesy shown to them.'

§ In fact, the German fleet at Scapa Flow was not scuttled until June 21 1919, after Raskolnikov's return to Russia.

language. He proudly replied that he knew none, and that he considered it quite unnecessary to trouble himself to learn any, since all foreigners ought to speak English. These words were uttered with a certain air of national arrogance.

The weather stayed fine all day. The sea was calm. Comrade Nynyuk and I strolled about the deck, chatting and enjoying the beauty of the blue sea. We dined below, in the NCOs' quarters, but separated from all the crew. We had no money at all, and so could not purchase any 'extras'. However, Comrade Nynyuk, not knowing English, agreed to accept some dish that was offered to him, even though it was not included in the official menu. A misunderstanding occurred. When, later, we were asked to pay for this dish, we found ourselves in an awkward situation, since we had no means of paying. The NCO in charge said, with a sour look, that the sum involved was not large and he would pay it.

At Copenhagen we were transferred to a British destroyer, and lodged in the corridor of the officers' quarters, beside the wardroom. There we spent the night swinging in string beds hung up like hammocks. They served our food at the officers' table, and we now sampled for the first time some English national dishes: at lunch we were given 'toast', that is, bread fried in butter [sic], and at tea we had marmalade.

Most of our time we spent on the top deck. The destroyer was travelling at full speed, raising behind it a foam-mound of seething water. One evening, before sunset, we saw on our starboard bow the pointed Gothic steeples of the Reval churches of Saint Olai and Saint Nicholas: the patterned tower of the Town Hall, like a minaret, gleamed for a moment, and the tall cranes of the Russo-Baltic Works stood out blackly against the sky.

After passing between Surop and Nargen Island, when the destroyer had the port of Reval on its beam it turned to port and began a northward course. Soon we could see the outline of Sveåborg Fortress. After passing Sveåborg so close that it was possible to make out distinctly not only the guns but even the expressions on the faces of the Finnish soldiers, we entered Helsingfors roadstead and drew alongside. Before we were allowed to go ashore, all our belongings were searched. They took away my big collection of cuttings from the British press. Manuscripts were let through. The British were motivated in their confiscation of the cuttings by the wartime law called 'Dora' which prohibited the export of printed matter. But the war with Germany was over. Evidently the law retained its force because Britain, without having declared war on us, was actually carrying on military operations against Soviet Russia, seen by capitalist Britain as an enemy country.* After this search, Comrade Nynyuk and I were taken ashore and put into a guardhouse, a small, one-storeyed building on the quay, near the Mariinsky Palace.†

Early next morning we were led out into the street. Kodaks clicked amid the rays of the rising sun. The photographers included Finnish officers. They took us by car to the railway station and sat us in a third-class compartment. The tall, dry Finnish officer who had been assigned as escort looked at us with unconcealed hatred and addressed us roughly and haughtily. The representative of the British consulate in Helsingfors and the plenipotentiary of the Danish Red Cross, who accompanied us to the frontier, were indignant at this attitude on the part of the Finns and insisted on moving us into a 'soft' carriage. The train started off that evening. We soon fell asleep and did not realise that we had reached the Finnish frontier station till we awoke in the morning. Accompanied by the British and Danish officials and escorted by Finnish soldiers we walked, carrying our suitcases, towards the long-desired Soviet frontier. The weather was clear and sunny. My joyful excitement saved me from noticing how heavy my suitcase was.

---

* The war with Germany was not officially over until the peace treaty was signed, on June 28 1919.

† There was no 'Mariinsky Palace', officially so called, in Helsingfors (Helsinki). The guardhouse was opposite the Emperor's (now the President's) Palace, across Mariinskaya Street.

We quickly covered the distance between the Finnish frontier station and Byeloostrov. At last we beheld Byeloostrov railway station, with its huge red placard turned towards Finland and inscribed 'Death to Butcher Mannerheim!' In front of the station was a small wooden bridge with handrails, over the river Sestra. We were ordered to halt at this bridge, before the lowered frontier-barrier. I put my suitcase down on the ground, took off my hat and, with relief, wiped the sweat from my brow.

XXII

How my heart began to beat when, on the Soviet side of the bridge, I saw fluttering in the wind the cap-ribbons of Red sailors. The brass instruments of a band shone brightly in the sunlight. On the Soviet side a group of men approached the bridge: they were dressed in green British jackets, with on their heads pancake-shaped caps from which long peaks projected.* The thick-set Finnish officer who was in charge of the exchange ceremony ordered that the barrier be lifted, and then advanced to the middle of the bridge. The Soviet frontier-barrier was also lifted, and, one after the other, the British officers began to walk towards Finland. First came Major Goldsmith, an officer of royal blood,† the head of the British Mission in Caucasia, who had been arrested at Vladikavkaz. Broad-shouldered, tall and dark, he crossed into Finnish territory and looked at me with curiosity, saluting in the military manner. I raised my felt hat and gave a slight bow. When eight or nine British officers had crossed the frontier, our sailors began to protest. A doubt had arisen in their minds: were the Finnish officers perhaps going to cheat them and, after getting all the British prisoners into

---

* According to a Soviet documentary publication, the British prisoners were escorted by Larissa Reissner. She died in 1926, having left Raskolnikov for Radek some years earlier.

† According to the Royal Archives at Windsor Castle there is no evidence that Major G.M. Goldsmith (who had taken over command of 'Caumilage' — the Caucasus Military Agency — after the shooting of Colonel Pike) had any connection with the royal family, and there is nothing to suggest this in the papers concerning him in the Foreign Office and War Office archives.

Red Navy sailors go into battle against Yudenich — the first fight Raskolnikov faced on his return to Soviet Russia

Finland, make off with me? They demanded that I be at once sent across into Soviet territory. But the Finns were adamant. They did not trust our men, either, and feared that after I had crossed the frontier the exchange would immediately be stopped, and the remaining British officers left un-exchanged. After brief negotiations, the two sides arrived at a compromise. It was decided to put Comrade Nynyuk and me in the middle of the bridge, so that when the last of the British had passed us, we could then complete our walk across the frontier. Hardly had we set foot on the bridge than the band on the Soviet side began to play, loudly and triumphantly, the *International*. The Finnish officers, taken by surprise, were confused and did not know what to do. Fortunately, they were rescued from their embarrassment by the British. The latter, as though in response to an order, all, at once, raised their hands to the salute. Following their example, the polished Finnish officers hesitatingly and unwillingly lifted their hands, tightly enclosed in white gloves, with their arms slackly bent at the elbow, and touched their elegant helmets, which, with their close-fitting uniforms, made them look like pre-war Prussian officers.

When all the British were on the bridge, we crossed into Soviet territory. Boundless joy gripped me when, after five months in prison, I found myself once more in the socialist fatherland. I greeted the comrades and thanked the sailors for coming to meet me. They all greeted me and expressed amazement at how highly Bolsheviks were rated on the world market. Just think! Two Bolsheviks had been exchanged for nineteen British officers.* It turned out that the British, who had at first demanded in exchange for us one naval officer and four sailors, later started to act like merchants surprised at finding that their goods are in demand in the bazaar. Like the trading nation they are, the British raised the price until, at last, not stopping at the figure of nineteen British officers, they

---

* The number of British personnel exchanged for Raskolnikov and Nynyuk was eighteen. There were eight officers, three NCOs, three private soldiers and four civilians. Their names appeared in the *Times* of May 30 1919.

demanded in addition, two Russian White-Guard generals.*
This insolence exasperated the People's Commissar of Foreign
Affairs, and he threatened to break off negotiations. The British
then 'yielded' and gave up their demand for the White-Guard
generals, agreeing to be satisfied with nineteen of their own
officers.

Among those who met me at Byeloostrov was our Finnish
comrade, now dead, Ivan Rakhiya. He offered to take me to
Petrograd by car, but I made the journey by rail. At Byeloostrov station our Red frontier-guards asked me to share with
them my impressions of Western Europe, and from the platform of the carriage I delivered a short speech about the international situation. I devoted particular attention to the intervention against the USSR and to the 'peace' talks at Versailles,
which were pregnant with the danger of a new war.†

That evening, on arrival at Petrograd, I went to see Comrade
Zinoviev. In his apartment in the Hotel Astoria I met Comrade
Stalin, who had just come from Moscow, on account of the
immediate threat to Lenin's city.§

It was May 27 1919. Helped by the British fleet, Yudenich
was launching his first attack on one of the most revolutionary
cities in the world.

---

* The voluminous correspondence in the Foreign Office archives concerning the
exchange of prisoners contains no mention of any 'White-Guard generals'. The Soviet
side had, however, engaged in some 'oriental bargaining' of a somewhat macabre kind.
In his message of January 24 1919 Chicherin had proposed that, in exchange for British
subjects in Soviet hands, not only Raskolnikov and Nynyuk but also Shaumyan,
Djaparidze and the rest of the 26 Baku commissars be returned to Russia — this
although, as the British Foreign Office noted, the Soviet wireless had reported on
November 16 1918 that these men had been 'killed by the White Guards' (FO
371/3938/26748).

† The mention of Versailles, 'pregnant with the threat of a new war', is omitted in the
1964 edition.

§ In the 1936 edition the reference to Zinoviev is omitted and the paragraph begins:
'That evening, on arrival in Petrograd, I met at the Hotel Astoria Comrade Stalin,
who . . .' In the 1964 edition the entire paragraph is omitted, thus avoiding mention of
both Zinoviev and Stalin.

The Taking of Enzeli

I

Sergo Ordjonikidze* lived in Baku on Freedom Square, not far from the tomb of those who died for the revolution.

The entrance to his flat was from a small but quite elegant yard. The spacious, well-lit rooms, with a glass-fronted veranda, were meagrely furnished and seemed empty. Evidently, the previous owner of the flat, who lived there in the Musavatist† period, had managed to make off somewhere with his furniture. The strong wooden floorboards shone with fresh, bright-yellow wax, but this renovation of the floor did not make the flat cosy: it was like a soldiers' bivouac. Sergo's rooms served as headquarters for the Party workers and those engaged in Soviet and military work in Baku. Morning and evening alike, the place was crowded with people, and the piercing sound of the telephone-bell rang out unceasingly.

A large group assembled every evening round the tea-table, covered with flower-patterned oilcloth. Tea was dispensed by Ordjonikidze's cordial, welcoming wife, a simple, kindly woman who looked after Sergo with maternal care.

That warm spring evening of May 16, 1920, when we sat at Sergo's tea-table, he was visited by Nariman Narimanovich Narimanov — swarthy-faced, with a big bald patch and eyes

---

* Ordjonikidze was at this time head of the Caucasian Bureau of the Central Committee of the Bolshevik Party.

† The Musavatists were the Azerbaidjani Moslem nationalists who came to power after the Turkish occupation of Baku in September 1918, remained in power under the British occupation, and survived until overthrown by the Bolsheviks in April 1920.

116

dark as prunes. He was the Chairman of the Council of People's
Commissars of the Azerbaidjan Soviet Republic, and he had
just returned from Moscow. I looked at the clock: it would soon
be the time appointed for us to weigh anchor. I got up from the
table and said my goodbyes.

'Well, comrade, I wish you success,' said N.N. Narimanov,
with an affectionate glance from his deep-set dark eyes. Flushed
with emotion, Sergo Ordjonikidze uttered, loudly, warmly and
cheerfully, some kind words of farewell. We embraced and
kissed each ,other.

From Sergo and Narimanov I received my final instructions
from the Party and Government of Soviet Azerbaidjan.* After
taking leave of them I emerged from the house, got into the
long, open motor-car which was waiting for me at the gate — a
vehicle which had withstood much battering in the sandy
wastes of Astrakhan during the civil war — and set off towards
the naval harbour. My skilful driver, Astafyev, a big-built,
broad-shouldered sailor who seemed to be knitted together
from nothing but muscles, conveyed me quickly in this rickety
machine through the dark, dimly-lit streets of Baku. After
passing the maritime boulevard, which was lit by high, suspended lamps, the car, now in third gear, tore along Baku's
endless quayside in the direction of Cape Bailov, surrounded

---

* When the entire 'Russian' coast of the Caspian Sea had been occupied by the
Bolsheviks, the White-Guard fleet withdrew to the Persian port of Enzeli, where it was
interned. The Soviet Government was concerned to take over these ships, so as to
ensure unimpeded movement of oil from Baku to Astrakhan and from there up the Volga
to Moscow and Petrograd. With the Donets Basin coalfield still in ruins as a result of
the civil war, supplies of oil were of vital importance for fuel and heating. On April 20,
1920, Trotsky wrote to Lenin and Chicherin: 'With reference to Raskolnikov's enquiry
. . . as to how to deal with the White fleet at Enzeli, I propose sending the following
instruction: "The Caspian must be cleared of the White fleet at all costs. If a landing on
Persian territory is required, it must be carried out . . .' (*The Trotsky Papers*, Vol.II,
1971, p.147). On May 1 the Volga-Caspian Flotilla, commanded by Raskolnikov,
arrived at Baku, and was renamed the Caspian Fleet. On May 9 Raskolnikov was
appointed commander of the fleet of Soviet Azerbaidjan, which was at this stage
formally a separate state from Soviet Russia. On May 14 the commander-in-chief of
Soviet Russia's naval forces, A.V. Nemitz, ordered Raskolnikov to seize the White
ships.

by hills that showed dark in the distance. Somewhere to the right the sharp silhouette of a slender minaret was glimpsed for a moment.

On arriving at the naval harbour I went aboard the destroyer *Karl Liebknecht*, which was lying by the sea-wall, and ordered that the anchor be weighed. It was dark, the inhabitants of the port were already asleep, and the departure of our squadron could pass unnoticed, at least till dawn came.

The steam-winches hissed, the bell of the engine telegraph rang, the heavy iron links of the anchor-chain crashed down, and the destroyer began, smoothly and slowly, to move off from the stone sea-wall. We sailed slowly past the flickering beacon light on Nargen Island, and out into the pitch-black darkness of the Caspian night.

II

The hot southern sun flooded with its light the boundless blue expanse of the Caspian Sea. The steel hull of the destroyer *Karl Liebknecht* shuddered rhythmically. Thick clouds of black smoke poured out of the ship's wide funnels and were carried away by the wind.

Coal-dust crunched like sand under one's feet on the slippery iron deck. On the forecastle and the quarterdeck the four-inch guns drowsed beneath their covers of unbleached canvas. Amidships, along the hull, stretched out the long snouts of the torpedo-tubes, charged with Whitehead torpedoes, that gleamed in the sunshine like gigantic silver cigars. The other destroyers followed *Liebknecht* in orderly line-ahead formation. On the flanks of this joint flotilla of the RSFSR and the Azerbaidjan navies the single-funnel gunboats *Kars* and *Ardahan*, which possessed only slight stability, tossed rhythmically in the swell.

In the midst of our squadron, covered on all sides by warships, was the high-boarded oil-tanker which carried Kozhanov's landing-party.

Ordjonikidze

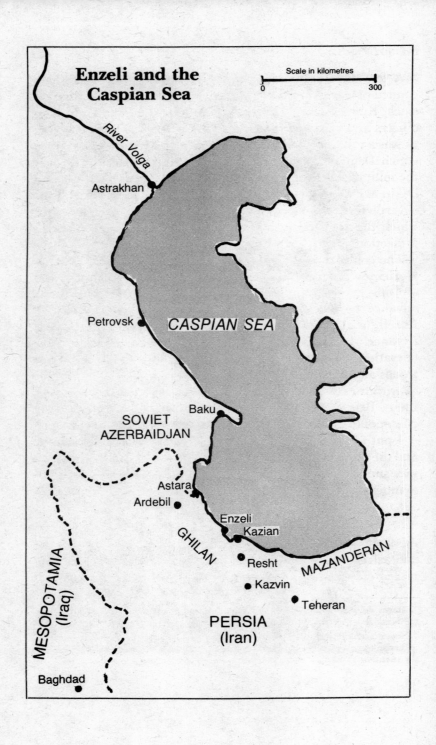

**Enzeli and the
Caspian Sea**

Scale in kilometres

0   300

River Volga

Astrakhan

Petrovsk

CASPIAN SEA

Baku

SOVIET
AZERBAIDJAN

Astara

Ardebil

Enzeli

GHILAN

Kazian

Resht

MAZANDERAN

Kazvin

Teheran

MESOPOTAMIA
(Iraq)

PERSIA
(Iran)

Baghdad

A few days before the expedition set out we had held a council of war. Along with the chief of staff, Vladimir Andreyevich Kukel,* quick, lively and slim as a boy, all the flag-officers and ships' commanders were present. The task before us was a raid on Enzeli, in order to seize the White-Guard fleet which Denikin's henchmen had taken thither and to recover the military equipment they had carried off from Petrovsk and Baku. We knew that there were British troops at Enzeli but, nevertheless, we were determined to get back the property with which the Denikinites had made off to Persia, under British protection.

The commander of the expeditionary force, Ivan Kuzmich Kozhanov, a tense young man, lean, with high cheekbones and slanting eyes narrow as slits, urged strongly that our troops advance by land, along the Caspian coast from Astara to Enzeli, with the flotilla providing a flank-guard to their advance. I disagreed with this plan. The purpose of our operation dictated speed and surprise. An advance by our troops along the Caspian shore would allow the White Guards to withdraw their booty into the interior of the country, and their British allies to bring up reinforcements from Mesopotamia and the South of Persia.†

I put forward my plan for a maritime expedition to Enzeli and the landing of a task-force very close to the town. This plan was supported by the majority of the flag-officers and commanders.

III

At dawn on May 18, when the Persians and the British were still asleep, our squadron suddenly appeared before the flat-roofed clay-and-gravel houses of Enzeli. Through binoculars

---

* This is the same Kukel with whom Raskolnikov had worked at Novorossiisk when the Black Sea Fleet was scuttled.

† However, the landing from the sea was, in fact, accompanied by a military invasion of Persian territory from Astara, and occupation of Ardebil. This was intended to divert the attention of the British commander from the naval operation.

one could make out the Governor's palace standing by the shore, surrounded by banana-trees and the umbrella-like tops of slender palms. To the left of Enzeli stretched the military town of Kazian, with its barracks, depots and long, one-storey buildings. The two narrow masts of a wireless station stood out sharply against the clear, turquoise-blue sky. Drawing near to Enzeli, my destroyer passed along the shore.

To the east of Enzeli and Kazian some heavy six-inch guns came into the field of view of my Zeiss binoculars. They were standing on the open sandy shore, without any artificial covering. No men were to be seen.

After choosing a suitable spot for our landing, I ordered that the signal be hoisted for the operation to begin.

A south wind was blowing, and the multi-coloured flags* fluttered and strove to fly away northward. The swell rocked our vessels rhythmically and rolled them from side to side.

Soon the first launches set forth from the black oil-tanker, which rose high above the water-line. The Red sailors, in blue jumpers with white collars, their long cap-ribbons streaming in the wind, rowed vigorously, straining their powerful muscles. But the launches were slow to reach the shore. The ebb-tide was pulling them out to sea. At last some of the sailors, in high-topped leather boots and gripping their brown rifles, leapt briskly on to the sands. A large red flag with the crossed-hammer-and-sickle emblem fluttered in their grasp like a huge bird. These men who had got ashore climbed the telegraph poles with their usual deftness and agility and cut the parallel copper wires that stretched between them. Enzeli's telegraphic communication with the outside world had been severed.

The sailors next occupied the causeway running from Enzeli to Resht and Teheran. Enzeli was cut off. Past the grim-looking but strangely silent guns I sailed towards Kazian and loosed off a few shots, so as to awaken the British from their placid

---

* By 'the multi-coloured' flags Raskolnikov presumably means the red, white and blue British flags.

slumbers. As we did not wish to destroy the houses, fragile and inflammable as straw, of the peaceful population of Enzeli, we concentrated our gunfire entirely on the military town of Kazian.

Out of the town a line of soldiers emerged, and quickly drew close to our landing party. These were brave and warlike Gurkhas from the independent Indian state of Nepal. Their heads were enclosed in snow-white turbans [*sic*]* as though bandaged with cheesecloth. From *Karl Liebknecht*'s two guns we began to fire on the advancing line. After a few overs which fell we knew not where, far off in the jungle, our shells began to fall short of the target, raising tremendous splashes in the water. At last we achieved a hit: our shells now fell close to the line of soldiers, sending black columns of earth and smoke into the sky.

By all the rules of higher mathematics, the soldiers had been caught, without realising it, in a bracket, and were being subjected to annihilating gunfire. 'On the line of soldiers, rapid fire. Range 28, deflection 2,' I ordered, and my order, quickly transmitted by the red flags of the signallers, ran through the ships of our squadron like an electric current. All the ships, as though celebrating, opened a rapid and deafening cannonade.

Hell broke loose on land. Our shells threw up all the earth around the Indian soldiers. But the swarthy Gurkhas in their snow-white turbans continued to press on along the narrow spit of sand, enclosed on one side by the sea and on the other by marshes and ponds. There was no cover for them there and nowhere for them to manoeuvre. The generals who had sent

---

* The Soviet landing was indeed opposed by a company of the 1st/2nd Gurkha Rifles, but one is surprised to read of Gurkha troops going into battle wearing turbans. (Later, Raskolnikov writes of 'Gurkhas and Sikhs', but neither of the other two Indian infantry units of 36 Brigade stationed in this area — the 1st/42nd Deoli Regiment and the 122nd Rajputana Infantry — appears to have included any Sikhs.)

   The Soviet attack began at 5.15a.m. and the bombardment lasted for an hour and a half. Two of the Gurkha soldiers were killed and six wounded. The total number of British-commanded troops at Enzeli was about 500, while the Soviet forces amounted to more than 1,500 men.

them into battle looked on them as cannon-fodder and cruelly urged them on to certain, inevitable death.

Despite the destructive fire from all our vessels, the British officers did not order their men to retreat. And this was not courage but foolishness.

Eventually, when the frequent shell-bursts physically barred their path, the Nepalese riflemen faltered and fled. After this initial defeat of the British troops, the telegraphist on duty brought me from the wireless cabin a despatch he had just received and hastily written out in pencil. The British general, frightened by the retreat of the brave Indian soldiers in white turbans, was asking me, with delightful belatedness, what the purpose was of this visit by the Red Navy. The radiogram, in English, was signed by Brigadier-General Champain.*

I replied that the Red Navy had no aggressive intentions either towards the British troops or towards the Persian Government. Our purpose was to recover the ships and military equipment stolen by Denikin's men from Soviet Azerbaidjan and Soviet Russia. So as to avoid any misunderstandings I proposed to the British commander that he immediately withdraw his troops from Enzeli.

The luckless British commander now entered into wireless correspondence with me. 'By whose authority have you come here?' he asked: a ticklish and somewhat indelicate question.

'The Soviet Government bears no responsibility for me. I have come here on my own initiative, on my own responsibility and at my own risk,' I answered proudly.

The British general said that, as he had no power to sur-

---

* Brigadier-General H.F. Bateman-Champain was relieved of his command as a result of the Enzeli affair. In 1922 he became Secretary-General of the British Red Cross Society, a position he held until his death in 1933. Field-Marshal Lord Ironside, who took over from Champain in October 1920, writes rather sarcastically about his predecessor's regime, mentioning that the commander 'had been allowed . . . to have his wife and family of two children and a European nurse up with him in Kazvin. The Indian troops had a good deal of their heavy kit with them, including band instruments. All seemed to be a happy party.' (*High Road to Command*, 1972, pp.128-129.) Champain happened to be at Enzeli on May 18 because he had come to witness the test-firing of the newly-installed shore batteries.

render Enzeli, he was seeking instructions from Sir Percy Cox, the High Commissioner in Mesopotamia.* Until a reply had been received from Baghdad, General Champain proposed that hostilities be called off and a truce concluded.

The slight wind and the swell slowed down the disembarkation of our men. There were no waves, but the light launches bobbed up and down like nutshells on the water and could be rowed only slowly and with difficulty to the low, sloping beach.

It was to our advantage to gain time, and so I agreed to a truce, adding that I gave the British two hours for their talks with Baghdad.

Struggling desperately against the swell and the wind, the expeditionary force continued to disembark. The sloping sandy spit was black with sailors. The continuous increase in the strength of our forces on the shore seriously alarmed the British commander. We received another wireless message. Referring to the truce which had been concluded, General Champain requested that there be no further landings by our men.

Recalling with difficulty the words of English I had acquired in my time behind the bars of Brixton Prison, I somehow composed a reply in the alien language. I brought it to the notice of General Champain that a truce meant cessation of direct military operations, but did not in the least exclude preparing for such operations. The British general evidently realised that further argument was useless and gave no reply.

IV

Soon we made out through our binoculars a torpedo-boat approaching us very rapidly from the direction of Enzeli Bay.

---

* Cox was at this time Britain's Minister in Teheran. He was not transferred to Baghdad until June 1920. Even so, Champain had difficulty in contacting him, as Raskolnikov had cut the telegraph wires. He appears to have tried to get through, with much delay, first by motoring to Resht and telegraphing Teheran from there, and then by sending an aeroplane to Teheran. (He had a radio transmitter, but it broke down.)

The vessel's hull shuddered and shook like a man suffering
from St Vitus's dance. Her bow was high in the air and her
stern low down in the water. Behind her a great heap of
snow-white foam was raised by her powerful screw. A square
white flag flew from her mast, and was being blown in every
direction by the wind. The torpedo-boat drew alongside *Karl
Liebknecht* and a tall young officer in a greenish British service-
jacket with silver aiguillettes on his chest and narrow, khaki
shoulder-straps, made his way cautiously, clutching the hand-
rail, from the British vessel up on to the higher deck of our
destroyer. This was the *parlementaire* sent by the general.*

'Lieutenant Crutchley,' he said, introducing himself with a
polite salute. I gave him my hand. The young lieutenant's lips
were quivering. He was obviously concerned at finding himself
on a ship belonging to the dreaded Bolsheviks. I invited him
into my cabin. He cautiously descended the shaky ladder and
removed his cap, which was broad and round, like a pancake.
His fair hair was smooth, with a side parting. His youthful,
un-whiskered face was covered with a sickly pallor and looked
like parchment.

I asked him to sit down. For lack of a chair he sat on the bunk,
which was covered with a thick grey blanket.

'General Champain has told me to ask what it is you want,'
the lieutenant asked me in broken Russian, adjusting his neat,
spick-and-span jacket.

'Only one thing — withdrawal by the British troops, so that
we may, without hindrance, evacuate to Baku our military
property which was seized and carried off by the White
Guards,' I replied.

The British officer undid two massive gold buttons embossed
with eagles and produced from a side pocket of his elegant

---

* In his articles in the Vladikavkaz *Kommunist* of May 30 1920 and the *Petrogradskaya
Pravda* of July 15 1920 Raskolnikov says that Crutchley was accompanied by the
Governor of Enzeli, which contradicts his statement later in this narrative that he was
not visited by the Governor. Larissa Reissner, who accompanied Raskolnikov on this
expedition, also tells how the Governor came aboard and had a discussion with her
husband.

jacket a slim notebook, in which, with a small yellow pencil he extracted from a black casing, he wrote down my words verbatim.

'Will you let me send a telegram to my general?' he asked.

'Please do.'

We both returned to the top deck. The torpedo-boat on which the British lieutenant had arrived had already disappeared. I summoned the wireless operator and gave him the message that the lieutenant had composed.

Our destroyer rocked monotonously.

'I don't feel well. I feel sick,' confessed Lieutenant Crutchley, embarrassed and pale as a starched shirt. I invited him to go below and lie down on my bunk. He readily followed my advice.

'I'm surprised that you suffer from seasickness,' I remarked ironically, when we were down in the cabin. 'After all, the British are a seagoing nation, and usually feel at home on the sea.'

Lieutenant Crutchley was nonplussed and made no reply. After resting a while on the hard Bolshevist bunk, he pulled himself together somewhat.

'Tell me, please,' I said to him, when I saw that he was feeling better: 'did our visit today come as a surprise?'

'A complete surprise,' the young man frankly acknowledged. 'In the first few days after you took Baku we did indeed expect to see the Red Navy, and even got ready for that event, but now, after three weeks of peace and quiet, we had calmed down and decided that you were not going to come.' He smiled bitterly.

'General Champain, our brigade commander, normally lives at Kazvin, where he has his headquarters,' he added after a brief meditation. 'The general came to Enzeli to carry out an inspection, and suddenly got caught up in this affair.'

'Yes, it's a disagreeable business,' I said, sympathetically. I was happy that the presence in Enzeli of this general, who had accidentally fallen into a trap, was hastening the British surrender. If he had been sitting in the deep rear, without danger to his own life, the general would have issued warlike orders and made his men go to their deaths, but, as things were, he was obliged to save his own skin. That would make him tractable, I thought. Lieutenant Crutchley told me he had twice landed at Baku, with General Dunsterville, and fought against the Reds.*

'By the way, I should like to ask you a great favour,' he said, suddenly turning to me after a short pause. 'You see, I got married when I was in Baku — to a Russian girl, of course. She is charming. We set ourselves up in a comfortable flat in Enzeli, bought some expensive furniture, a grand piano and a bath. The piano cost me a terrible lot of money — and in this barbarous country they don't make decent musical instruments: but I couldn't refuse it to my wife, she plays so divinely. Now I'm afraid that, if we quit Enzeli, the piano will be left behind, and go to rack and ruin. Could you help me get my piano and my bath out of Enzeli?'

I found it hard not to laugh. At such a decisive moment as this the lieutenant was worried most of all about his petty-bourgeois comforts.

I promised that the piano and the bath would be evacuated next day, on a lorry going to Resht. Crutchley could not thank me too much for my courtesy: he calmed down and cheered up quite remarkably. Even his seasickness seemed to trouble him less.

Confused, stammering and trying hard to find words, he started to tell me, in a vague and contradictory way, but with great animation, about his origins in a very ancient and noble Scottish family. '"Crutch" means a cross, and "ley" is an old Scots word meaning a place where two roads intersect.'

'So, then, Crutchley means a cross at a crossroads,' I translated in a rough-and ready way.

---

* Presumably Crutchley had gone to Baku with 'Dunsterforce' in August 1918 and fought against the Turks who were attacking the city, and then had returned to Baku in November 1918 with General Thomson's 'Norperforce', after the Turkish surrender.

'Yes, that's right!' said the British officer, nodding his head happily.

I yawned and looked at my watch. The truce-period was nearing its end. I climbed up the sooty iron ladder to the top deck. After the stuffy cabin the strong salty wind off the sea refreshed me pleasantly. I ordered the landing-party to take the offensive and had the guns loaded. The black silhouettes of our sailors, like shadows on a Chinese screen, began to stir and move about on the shore. The grey steel guns fired a deafening salvo, softly slid back, and then resumed their former position. An oblong shell, with a conical point, cut through the air over Kazian with a piercing whistle and splashed down, without exploding, in some malarial swamp.

The British artillery remained silent. Encouraged by its inaction, we shot off a few more three-inch shells, ranging over Kazian, where General Champain and his staff were sitting, as though caught in a mousetrap. Our line of men moved quickly along the sandy shore. The Gurkhas in white turbans were nowhere to be seen. All of a sudden there rushed headlong up out of my cabin on to the top deck the scion of an ancient Scottish family, carrying in his hand his broad, pancake-like cap.

'For pity's sake, you can't do this,' the red-faced Crutchley protested, breathless with emotion. 'Here I am, a guest on your ship, and at the same time you are firing on the British. Let me go at once, and then do whatever you like, but while I'm here, stop firing.'

I soothed the distressed lieutenant and explained to him that, until his torpedo-boat arrived, I possessed, unfortunately, no means of getting him ashore. I declined to stop firing, pointing out that the truce had expired.

At that moment the wireless operator on duty gave me a message received from the shore station. General Champain complained that our units had destroyed all the telegraph lines, and so had made it difficult for him to communicate with the outside world. Consequently he had not yet obtained an answer

from Sir Percy Cox in Baghdad. In conclusion, Champain
proposed that the truce be extended for another hour.

We had not yet managed to put ashore the whole of our
expeditionary force, so that Champain's proposal was accept-
able. When Lieutenant Crutchley learnt that the truce was to
be extended, he sighed with relief, adjusted the silver aiguillettes on his chest, assumed a dignified air, and cheered up.

General Champain did not make use of the whole period
allowed him. Before the time laid down for the truce had
elapsed, he sent another wireless message saying that, although
no answer had been received from the High Commissioner for
Mesopotamia, he agreed to hand over Enzeli to the Red Navy,
on condition that the troops of His Britannic Majesty would be
allowed to leave the town with their weapons. He asked that I
send a representative to discuss the technical aspects of the
surrender of the town, of the White-Guard fleet and of all the
military equipment we were after. Our task did not include
making war on the British. In so far as they had agreed to quit
Enzeli, our task was done.

V

I summoned Comrade Kozhanov to my destroyer. He was
wearing a service-jacket and on the side of his head a cap of
curly brown lamb's wool. His lean, high-cheekboned face
smiled broadly and his narrow, slanting eyes gleamed with
excitement; he was delighted with our victory. I asked him to go
ashore and negotiate with the British general about the conditions for the surrender of Enzeli.

A motor-launch, snorting and poisoning the air with the
heavy, stifling smell of petrol, moved away from the short ladder
of my destroyer. Ivan Kuzmich Kozhanov, erect in military
fashion, stood by the low side of the vessel, which barely rose
above the water, and, smiling cheerfully, with his wide mouth
stretched almost up to his ears, saluted, his straight, almost
wooden fingers slightly touching his lamb's-wool cap cocked at

a jaunty angle. He successfully carried out his military-dip-
lomatic mission. During his negotiations it turned out that all
the breech-blocks had been removed from the guns on the
White-Guard ships: the British had sent them to Resht. Comrade Kozhanov demanded that they be returned. General
Champain promised that this would be done. And, to be sure, a
few days later, when Enzeli was already decorated all over with
red flags, a British lorry brought to the town those heavy steel
breech-blocks, polished and gleaming in the sunshine. I have
nothing to say against the British General Champain: he honourably carried out all his undertakings.*

General Champain left Enzeli in a roomy, six-seater car. His
officers went off in small, badly-battered Fords. The swarthy
Gurkhas and Sikhs in white turbans departed on foot, morosely
driving before them the grey donkeys that pulled the carts
laden with their meagre baggage. The Denikinite officers,
naval and military, with their golden shoulder straps, fled in
boats to the depths of the bay, which went far back into the
mainland. Through swamps, rice-fields and jungles densely
entwined with lianas they got to Resht that evening.

When Lieutenant Crutchley learnt of the British withdrawal, he asked permission to spend the night on our
destroyer, so as to be able next day to pack his things and send
off his furniture, with the piano and the bath. Early next
morning, amid the still unwarming rays of the sun, we entered
the inner harbour of Enzeli. The landing-stage and quays were
densely covered with a motley crowd. Persians in tall, round
caps of black karakul, women in stifling black yashmaks that
drooped to the ground like elephants' trunks, sunburnt and
barefoot children, all were crammed between the spreading
palm-branches and the broad, light-green leaves of the banana
trees. I came down from the bridge. Crutchley stood beside me
on the forecastle. The approach to the landing-stage was

---

* Raskolnikov required that a British officer (Captain Storey) be left with him as a
hostage until the breech-blocks arrived, and this was done.

difficult, but after swinging about slowly and for a long time we managed to heave to at the mooring-line.

'Just see how base people are,' said Crutchley, indignantly, turning to me and suddenly flushing: 'in that crowd gathered on the pier I can see several Persian notables. Only yesterday they were bowing before me and humbly ingratiating themselves, yet now they turn away, or stare at me insolently as though they don't know me. It's disgusting.'

The destroyer tied up at the pier almost opposite the elegant palace of the Governor, above which flew an immense Persian flag showing the emblem of lion, sword and sun. The fleet lay in the harbour: over the high sides of the black oil-tankers the long barrels of naval guns showed grey. Seaplanes white as albatrosses lay on the shore with their long wings stretched out helplessly.

We secured much booty at Enzeli. Besides the naval ships and aeroplanes our trophies included numberless guns, machine-guns, shells and rifles, with stocks of cartridges. The British left behind for us in Kazian quantities of tinned meat, biscuits and rum.*

Soon I made my way into the town. Not far from the quay a colourful and noisy bazaar began. Along both sides of a narrow street stretched enless rows of vegetables, dried fruit, rice, poultry and meat. Further along, the street entered a cool darkness, covered with a roof of black and rotten planks. Here they sold teapots, brightly decorated with flowers, many-coloured cotton prints, striped silk gowns, and skull-caps embroidered with silver and gold. Amid the motley crowd little grey donkeys minced on their thin springy legs: they were laden with huge bundles of chopped-up firewood, tied down with cords on both sides and dragging heavily to the ground.

Beyond the bazaar the residential quarter began. Grey

---

* The Soviet booty amounted to ten auxiliary cruisers, seven transports and smaller vessels, over 50 guns, with 20,000 shells, six seaplanes, more than 20 ships and field wireless stations and much other equipment, together with large quantities of oil, cotton and other stores, abandoned by the British.

houses made of clay and gravel were hidden behind monotonous high walls that hemmed in narrow, crooked and filthy streets. Here and there one came upon dark, cramped shops. The majestic building of the bath-house, with wide stone steps and a round dome, resembled an ancient temple. In the street in front of the bath-house a cheery, grinning barber was scraping with a sharp razor the tough, unsoaped bristles from the yellowish-red face of a young Persian. After quickly looking round the town, I lunched in a modest restaurant by the shore, and then returned to my ship.*

VI

Next day, having previously made an appointment, I went to call on the local Persian Governor. He received me in his palace, under the flag of the sword-wielding lion and the radiant sun. In the garden a single palm-tree, set in the ground, like a sentry, right before the entrance, softly rustled its leaves, narrow and sharp as daggers.

The spacious room, its floor covered throughout with a green carpet with intricate arabesque patterns, was as desolate as an empty barn. At the far end stood some chairs. One of these barely managed to accommodate a stout, swarthy, black-haired man with a puffy face and fat, shiny cheeks. I introduced myself and explained the purpose of the Red Navy's visit to Enzeli.

The Governor's interpreter, who wore white trousers like dirty drawers, translated my words immediately. The Governor said nothing, but absent-mindedly passed his beads between his short, fleshy fingers and gloomily nodded his head.

An old servant, treading lightly and noiselessly on the carpet

---

* On May 19 Raskolnikov sent a telegram to Moscow in which he said: 'The Red Navy, having conquered the Caspian Sea for the Soviet Republic, sends greetings from its Red shores to the beloved leaders and Red knights of the international proletariat, Lenin and Trotsky. The population of Persia [sic], without distinction of classes, is acclaiming, in our person, Soviet Russia as the liberator of the Moslem East from the world bourgeoisie.'

with his soft slippers, brought us some thick coffee steaming in miniature porcelain cups on a silver tray.

'The weather is lovely today,' said the Governor, changing the subject.

I drank my coffee, rose and took my leave. As I shook the Governor's stiff, thick hand, I assured him that we had no intention of interfering in the internal affairs of the Persian state. A cunning expression flashed in his round, sad eyes. The interpreter showed me to the entrance of the palace.

I did not receive a return visit from the governor. That same night he fled to Teheran. Next morning the whole town was gaily decorated with newly-made, bright red flags. Enzeli was expecting Kuchik Khan, who had been hiding in the jungle. He was in those days a terror to the British. Semi-brigand, semi-revolutionary, a supporter of national liberation for Persia, he filled the British merchants and officers with fear, as he boldly swept down on their cars from the rocks of the mountain-pass between Kazvin and Teheran. Not a few Fords and other vehicles had he hurled down the slope into the deep chasm. Like the Robin Hood of legend, Kuchik Khan took property from the rich and distributed it among the poor peasants. Like the hero of English folklore he was fantastically elusive, and disappeared after his raids into the mountains and forests. The peasants provided him with food, drink and shelter.*

A motley crowd was densely arrayed along the whole shore and packed the narrow quadrangle of the landing stage, which rested on piles. The town was in an excited state of agonising expectation and anticipation of the triumphal entry of its distinguished guest. Kuchik Khan had not been to Enzeli for several years.

First there appeared a troop of sunburnt, black-haired Kurds, armed to the teeth with rifles, revolvers and daggers. These were his personal bodyguard. Then, following soon

---

* On Kuchik (or Kuchuk) Khan, see Trotsky, *How the Revolution Armed*, Vol.3 (1981), pp.377-378. He arrived in Enzeli on May 23 and met Raskolnikov.

after, Kuchik Khan himself arrived, accompanied by his henchmen, to be noisily greeted by the Persian crowd. Tall, well-built, handsome, with regular features, he advanced with his head uncovered. Long, dark, curly hair fell in luxuriant locks to his shoulders. His chest was closely faced with criss-crossing machine-gun belts. Wide trousers were tucked into pale-green puttees, fastened with white tapes: on his feet gleamed silver-embroidered slippers of untanned leather, with sharply turned-up toes. Slowly and gravely he moved up the street, exchanging greetings with the crowd in a manner that combined joy with dignity.

A few days later I received a telegram from Teheran. The chairman of Persia's council of ministers, Vossugh ed-Dowleh, an Anglophil and a creature of the British, asked me to pass on to the Soviet Government a message which was appended. This lengthy telegram contained the Persian Government's official protest against the Soviet landing at Enzeli. It was in this way that direct diplomatic relations began between the Soviet Government and Persia. Until then the Anglophil Government of Vossugh ed-Dowleh had not wished to know us. Soon, normal diplomatic relations were established between Soviet Russia and Persia, and Vossugh ed-Dowleh fled to Baghdad, under the warm wing of his British protectors.*

At the beginning of June General Champain's troops evacuated Resht, Kuchik Khan occupied the town with his men, transferred his headquarters thither, proclaimed a republic and set up a Council of People's Commissars and a Revolutionary War Council, and began to prepare for a march on Teheran.

I soon left the stormy Caspian Sea and went north, to join the Baltic Fleet. Kuchik Khan subsequently betrayed the revolution, while at the same time continuing to resist the forces of the Shah. One winter's night when there was a cruel frost, during a severe blizzard, he froze to death at the top of a high

---

* Vossugh ed-Dowleh resigned and left Teheran for Baghdad on June 24.

mountain pass. The Government forces who were pursuing
Kuchik Khan stumbled upon his frozen body. They cut off his
handsome curly head and presented it as a trophy to the Shah.*

---

* In his reply to the Persian note of protest, Chicherin said, on May 23, that Raskolnikov had taken action without orders 'from the central Soviet Government'. On
June 5 he informed Persia that Soviet Russian forces had been ordered to evacuate
Persian territory and territorial waters, and on June 20 he claimed that there were no
more Soviet Russian forces there: any Soviet forces still in Persia were in the service of
Soviet Azerbaidjan. (In fact, Soviet forces, fanning out from Enzeli, remained in
occupation of large parts of Ghilan and Mazanderan provinces until September 1921.)
An appeal by Persia to the League of Nations produced no response, and so the
Teheran Government set about coming to terms on a friendly basis with the Soviet
power. Bonar Law, Lord Privy Seal and Leader of the House of Commons, had stated
on May 20 1920, in reply to a question about the events in Enzeli: 'His Majesty's
Government are under no obligation under the Anglo-Persian Treaty.'

The consequences of the Enzeli incident were a great deal of recrimination within the
British Establishment and a sharp decline in Britain's prestige in the Middle East. *The
Times* wrote on May 20: 'The truth is that ministers still approach Middle Eastern
matters with the habit of mind induced by the War. They practise Gallipoli methods.
They incur enormous responsibilities with light-hearted eagerness, without counting
the cost, without reckoning up their resources, and without considering where they will
be if something unexpected happens.' On May 21 the paper published under the
headline 'British Prestige Involved', a piece that began: 'A correspondent familiar with
the Middle East writes: The seizure of the Persian port of Enzeli by Bolshevist troops is
a very menacing occurrence. It may have consequences which will set alight the
inflammable material strewn throughout the Middle East, from Anatolia to the
North-West Frontier of India.' And on May 22 *The Times* continued its attack thus:
'When His Majesty's Government think fit to enlighten the public about the Persian
situation, perhaps they will also explain how it comes to pass that a British force,
reported to be nearly 500 strong, has been garrisoning a Persian port for the past two
years. Had the War Office forgotten its existence?'

The reproach to the War Office was misdirected. Already on February 11 1920 the
War Minister, Churchill, had urged the Cabinet to withdraw the garrison from Enzeli
'in order to escape the loss of prestige involved in a retirement in contact with the
enemy', and the Chief of the Imperial General Staff, Sir Henry Wilson, noted in his
diary on May 19, regarding the events at Enzeli: 'A nice state of affairs, which will have
a *bad* effect in the East. For months I have been begging the Cabinet to allow me to
withdraw from Persia and from the Caucasus. [There was still a British garrison in
Batum at this time — B.P.] Now perhaps they will.' The minister mainly responsible
for resisting the War Office proposals was the Foreign Secretary, Lord Curzon.
Churchill wrote to him on May 20 to protest against a policy of 'leaving weak British
forces tethered in dangerous places where they can be easily and suddenly over-
whelmed. I do not see that anything we can do now, within the present limits of our
policy, can possibly avert the complete loss of British influence throughout the
Caucasus, Transcaspia and Persia. If we are not able to resist the Bolsheviks in these
areas, it is much better by timely withdrawals to keep out of harm's way and avoid
disaster and the shameful incidents such as that which has just occurred.' (Quotations
from R. H. Ullman, *Anglo-Soviet Relations, 1917-1921*, Vol.3, 'The Anglo-Soviet Accord',

1972, pp.300, 363, and Martin Gilbert, *Winston S. Churchill*, Vol.IV, Companion Part 2 [Documents] 1977, pp.1101-1102.)

At the beginning of 1920 Britain had seemed to be about to reduce Persia to the status of a protectorate, with British control of the country's finances and armed forces, by means of a treaty which was before the Persian Parliament. The Bolshevik landing at Enzeli 'shook Persian confidence in the ability of the British to defend Iran' (N.S. Fatemi, *Diplomatic History of Persia, 1917-1923*, 1952, p.78) and encouraged all the elements that were opposed to the Anglo-Persian treaty. The United States and France were both eager to weaken Britain's position in the Middle East, and the influence of their representatives, together with Persian national feeling, resulted, in the post-Enzeli circumstances, in repudiation of the treaty. British advisers and soldiers left Persia during 1921, and a treaty between Soviet Russia and Persia authorised Soviet forces to enter Persian territory in the event of the reappearance there of any forces hostile to the Soviet power. In the context of the time, that meant British forces. In 1941, however, it was by mutual consent that Soviet and British forces entered Persia, in order to facilitate communication between them and to frustrate pro-German activities inside the country.

For the background to the events in Persia in 1920-1921, see the article 'Persia I' in the *Central Asian Review*, Vol.IV, No.3 (1956); the proceedings of the *Congress of the Peoples of the East, Baku, September 1920* (New Park Publications, 1977); and J.M. Balfour, *Recent Happenings in Persia* (1922).

DPZ*

I

On that May evening I returned home late, just as usual. Tired out by my editorial work on *Pravda*, stunned by the constant ringing of the telephone, I went straight to bed and slept like a log. The night of May 21-22 1912 claimed its own.

I was awakened in the middle of the night by a loud voice asking sternly: 'Is your name Ilyin?' Opening my eyes, I saw an unfamiliar bearded face leaning over me. From his light-grey greatcoat with narrow silver shoulder-straps I deduced that this man must be a superintendent of police.

Around my cot, as though at a death-bed, there stood in a semicircle two policemen in black greatcoats with shoulder-straps of red braid, the caretaker of our block of flats, and a number of mysterious strangers, some wearing pea-green overcoats, others in long-skirted jackets.

'Is your name Ilyin?' the police official repeated, sternly.

'Yes, I'm Ilyin,' I replied, rubbing my eyes.

'Is your first name Fyodor?' he demanded, in the same unfriendly tone. And without waiting for my answer, he ordered me, crisply: 'Get dressed: we are searching your place.'

'But have you a warrant?' I asked.

'Of course,' the superintendent replied, and, dipping into a shabby, battered black briefcase, he produced and held out to me a piece of paper, folded in four. I looked at it and saw that it

---

* The initials of the Russian words for 'pre-trial detention centre'.

contained instructions to arrest me regardless of the results of the search.

With a feeling of bitterness I took up my clothes from the chair on which they lay and set about dressing. The noise in the room awakened my brother, a high-school boy, who slept in the same room with me.* At the same time, my mother rushed in.

It was about two in the morning. Apparently, the policemen had come to the door of our flat accompanied by the caretaker and witnesses, and had rung the bell. My mother had gone into the hallway and, without taking the hook off the door, asked, 'Who's there?' 'It's a telegram,' answered the familiar voice of the caretaker, and my mother, suspecting nothing, at once opened the door. She had not even been able to warn me of the arrival of our unwelcome visitors.

When I had put on my trousers of blue diagonal and, over my black sateen blouse, my student's jacket with the mono-grammed shoulder-straps, the superintendent demanded to know where I kept my things. I indicated my half of the room: my brother lived in the other half.

The gang that burst in upon us now got down to making a zealous search which went on from two until six. They rum-maged among all my things, just like burglars. They took all my correspondence from a drawer in the desk and carefully wrapped it in paper. But it was my extensive library that caused them particular concern. The policemen took out and put on one side every work that aroused their suspicions even slightly, and the superintendent, gravely assuming his pince-nez, attached to a long black cord, examined each item with care. He evidently believed in the principle that it is better to overdo things than to risk missing something, and so assigned for removal a big pile of books of a perfectly legal nature, including a thick work on problems of municipal economy which I had borrowed from the library of the Academy of Sciences. However, to this ignorant superintendent what

---

* At the time of these events Raskolnikov was 20 years old. His brother, known later as A.F. Ilyin-Zhenevsky, was 18.

seemed especially suspicious was anything in the form of a
pamphlet. Every pamphlet seemed to him to be seditious.
Amongst other items he confiscated the pamphlet, written by
the priest Grigory Petrov, before he was unfrocked,* entitled
God's Workers. It was the word 'workers' that had caught his
attention. I could not refrain from mirth at the spectacle of this
assiduity on the part of the Tsarist sleuth, and burst out laughing. Embarrassed, the superintendent left the pamphlet on my
desk.

Suddenly I remembered that in a side-pocket of my jacket
there was a compromising note written by a comrade of my
brother's, the 'Witmerist'† and Anarchist Vladimir Prussak.
In this note Volodya had warned me that intensified searches
and arrests were being carried out in the city. I had received the
note the previous day and, in the hurly-burly and haste of my
editorial work, had omitted to destroy it. I asked for permission
to go to the toilet. After a moment's hesitation, the superintendent gave me permission: though he told one of the
policemen to accompany me, he did not think to search me first.
I locked myself in the little toilet, while the policeman remained
in the corridor. I took the unlucky note out of my pocket and
tore it into small pieces, then joyfully pulled the handle and
flushed it away.

When I returned to my room the search was still in progress.
The superintendent, wearing his pince-nez again and seated, as
though in his own home, at my little desk, was earnestly, with
serious mien, making a list of the titles of the books, newspapers
and pamphlets to be removed.

'One issue of the newspaper *Za pravo*', he said aloud, dic-
tating to himself, and, fearing to make a mistake, slowly

---

* G.S. Petrov, a Petersburg priest who was a friend of Tolstoy's, criticised Tsardom
from a liberal standpoint in some of his numerous writings. In 1908 he was unfrocked
after sending a letter to Metropolitan Anton denouncing the degeneration of the
Orthodox Church into a tool of the autocracy.

† A secret conference of secondary-school students held at Witmer's High School for
Girls, in Petersburg, was raided by the police, who made 45 arrests.

inscribed one letter after another, like a schoolboy learning to write. Through his illiteracy, however, he did make a mistake. I had no newspaper called *Za pravo* (For justice): in fact, it was an issue of *Za partiyu* (For the Party), the Paris-published organ of the Bolshevik 'conciliators',* which had somehow accidentally arrived at the editorial office of *Pravda* and which I had taken home to read. Naturally, I did not correct the superintendent's mistake. At that moment I happened to notice, lying on the edge of the desk, the latest issue of our central organ, Lenin's *Sotsial-Demokrat*. The policemen had taken this newspaper out of the drawer in the desk and put it down where it could be seen. While the superintendent was busy recording the imaginary newspaper *Za pravo*, I discreetly pushed the copy of *Sotsial-Demokrat* aside, on to the low window-sill behind the desk. Printed on thin cigarette-paper, it slipped lightly and silently out of the window. Nobody had noticed my manoeuvre: every one of the policemen was ecstatically absorbed in his own particular task.

At last the search was over. The superintendent read out, solemnly and distinctly, the record of the search he had carried out: then, in a serious, decorous manner, as though performing a rite, he signed this record, making an extraordinarily complicated flourish under his name, after which he called upon the witnesses and me to sign it.

The witnesses — the detectives in their pea-green overcoats and the corn-chandlers in their long-skirted jackets — reverently, on tiptoe, approached the desk and affixed their signatures to the document with a grave air, as though they were taking part in a highly important and responsible affair which could not succeed without their co-operation.

The superintendent then turned to me and said: 'Bring your bedding with you.'

My mother wrapped the pillow in the blanket and carefully

---

* The 'conciliators' opposed the final split in the Social-Democratic Party, between the Bolsheviks and Mensheviks, which was accomplished in 1912.

tied up this awkward parcel with some string. I managed to shove a packet of books into the middle of it. Then I kissed my mother and my brother and, escorted by the policemen, went down the stairs.

When I reached the yard, which was like a deep well, I looked up and saw my mother and brother at our window on the second floor, waving their handkerchiefs in farewell to me as I set off for an unknown destination. I waved back to them and accompanied by the policemen, passed through the gate. At this early hour Simbirskaya Street was still quite deserted. It was already light. I carried my bundle under my arm. The pillow wrapped in a blanket, though not heavy, was bulky. The policemen lugged misshapen, awkward packages, wrapped in newspaper, containing the things they had taken from my place.

Our strange company thus consisted of a student, a superintendent of police and some policemen. The few passers-by shied away in alarm when they encountered this procession.

We walked to the white Tikhvinskaya church, turned left along Tikhvinskaya Street, and arrived at the dark and dirty police station. The policeman on duty, who was sitting dejectedly, in his greatcoat and cap, at a plain wooden table in a corner, jumped to his feet, straightened up, and saluted the superintendent.

II

I was taken into a separate room, unfurnished except for a table black with dirt and some long, dilapidated benches. A drunk was brought into the police station. He could not stand up and could only mumble indistinctly. A woman in prunella overshoes and with her multicoloured cotton skirt tucked up, came in, rattling a bucket, and applied herself to washing the painted plank floor. Soapsuds flowed over the yellow floorboards, but the charwoman caught them up adroitly with her wet cloth and squeezed the dirty water into her bucket. The superintendent went out and the policemen sat down at the table with the air of persons who had accomplished a difficult but extremely important task. They chatted cheerfully together and drank tea from thick earthenware mugs.

Although I had been arrested, and responsibility for my subsistence now lay not with me but with those who had arrested me, nobody concerned himself with my needs. While I was at the police station I was given neither water nor bread, though I felt faint from hunger and thirst.

I had to spend several hours in that place. When the working day began, the assistant chief of police arrived at the police station. This was Count Tatishchev, a former officer, with long, upward-twisted red moustaches: having lost his fortune at cards, he had been drummed out of some Guards regiment for dissipation and embezzlement. Tatishchev ordered that I be taken to the premises of the political police. In a cab, sitting beside a lean, freckled policeman who kept a firm grip on the black leather scabbard of his straight sword and was continually adjusting his revolver holster, I was taken across Sampsonievsky Bridge on to the Petersburg Side. There was by now much activity in the streets. Officials were hurrying to their offices and students and high-school boys to their classes. The curious sight of a student and a policeman amicably travelling together in the same cab attracted general attention, and evoked smiles from some, sympathetic glances from others, and from yet others a response of perplexity and incomprehension.

The thin cab-horse, its ribs sticking out, like a funeral nag deprived of its horsecloth, jogged along slowly.

While we were making our way in this leisurely fashion to the headquarters of the political police, my travelling companion kept pestering me with his complaints about the burdensomeness of service in the police. Trying to win my sympathy and push me into some openly political talk, the policeman, giving me sidelong looks from his sunken, colourless eyes, told me that he was paid very little, too little to keep his family on, and swore that he had long been in agreement with the

students and the socialists. Suspecting an attempt at provocation, I stayed silent as a fish.

The political police headquarters was situated at the corner
of Kronverksky and Aleksandrovsky Avenues, not far from the
Birzhevoy Bridge, in a small, two-storey building with iron
bars over the windows. Outwardly there was nothing to dis-
tinguish it from the adjoining houses and there seemed nothing
to betray the presence within of the most important organ of the
political police. There was no signboard anywhere. Through
the gateway my police escort led me into the office and handed
me over in exchange for a receipt, with the same cold indif-
ference with which a postman hands over telegrams and registered letters.

In the political police premises it was just as dark, dirty and
bleak as in the police station I had left. They sat me down in a
little room with a bare, unpainted floor. A tall, broad-
shouldered worker was there already. He came from the
Obukhov works and had been arrested that same night. He was
very worried about his wife and four children, whom his arrest
had left without anything to eat. Apart from two wooden stools
and a small table there was no furniture in our cell, not even
bunks.

At about mid-day they brought us lunch — soup and cutlets.
I had had nothing to eat since the morning and was furiously
hungry, so the lunch seemed to be remarkably tasty, and I said
something in praise of it.

'We get our lunches from a restaurant,' was the proud reply
of the policeman who was removing from the table, with his
stiff, red fingers, the empty, clattering trays.

III

Soon after this I was summoned for interrogation.

In a small room with curtains, at a desk which was unexpectedly placed just by the door, at right angles to the wall, sat a
young officer of the gendarmerie, his hair pomaded and

smoothly parted and with a clipped black moustache. On the starched shirt-cuffs that stuck out from the sleeves of his gendarmerie jacket I saw some elegant cufflinks in the form of small gold revolvers. He offered me a blank sheet of paper and his cigarette-case. I accepted the paper but declined the cigarette.

With exaggerated politeness but in a sort of malicious tone he put questions to me about my membership of the students' all-Petrograd joint committee and about my participation in the demonstration on the Nevsky Prospekt. To all his questions I replied in the negative.

'And do you know So-and-so?' The cavalry captain mentioned some name that meant nothing to me. 'No, I don't,' I replied.

After that he asked me whether I knew various other people, among whom were indeed some comrades of mine, but in the same bored monotone I answered that I knew none of them and was hearing their names for the first time.

After asking me an unexpected question about the Socialist-Revolutionary Party, my interrogator let me go back to my cell. It became clear to me that the gendarmes were groping their way: having arrested me, they were now striving to find some evidence to justify the arrest.

I had never had anything whatsoever to do with the Socialist-Revolutionary Party. The 'subjective' sociological method of Lavrov and Mikhailovsky, their failure to understand the mass movement of the working class, individual terror, repudiation of Marxism — all this repelled me from the petty-bourgeois SR Party. From the moment I began to concern myself with theory I had been an orthodox Marxist.

I did not belong, either, to the students' joint committee, which united the students of all the institutions of higher education in Petersburg, although I knew of the existence of this organisation.

I had indeed taken part in the demonstration on the Nevsky Prospekt. But my principal political activities had consisted in acting as secretary of *Pravda* and, along with Comrade V.M. Molotov, working in the Bolshevik group in the Polytechnical Institute. Yet the gendarmerie officer had not even hinted at those activities.

'Either he is in difficulties owing to lack of material or he is deliberately trying to catch me,' I thought, as I sat on a stool in my cell.

At this time it was the fashion among the gendarmes to 'catch' politicals by means of such an elementary method as this. A prisoner's mother, for example, would call on the colonel of gendarmerie and ask to be allowed a meeting with her son.

'Well, you know, your son is accused of belonging to the Socialist-Revolutionary Party,' the gendarme would say to her in a categorical tone.

'Oh, come, Colonel,' the mother would reply, in amazement: 'my son has always been a convinced Social-Democrat.'

The gendarme would rub his hands with glee. That was all he needed. Perhaps the captain, when he asked me questions about the SRs, expected me to become indignant and, in an outburst of uncontrollable feeling, acknowledge my actual Party membership. However, I had managed to keep control of myself. I had even gloated over the fact that the gendarme's inquiry was following a false trail.

There was nobody with whom I could share my thoughts and feelings. The thickset Obukhov worker made a favourable impression, but it was the first time I had seen him and I had no grounds for supposing I could be frank with him.

In any case, we were quickly separated. A gendarme entered the cell and ordered me to follow him. Clutching my pillow and blanket, I went out into the yard, where a covered carriage was standing with a pair of horses in the shafts. Sharing my seat in this carriage was a young, fair-haired man of extremely 'educated' appearance, wearing rimless pince-nez, a soft hat and a brand-new grey jacket.

The gendarme took the seat facing us, and our carriage set

off, creaking and rocking. By way of the Birzhevoy Bridge, the University Embankment and the Dvortsovy Bridge, we arrived at last in Voznesensky Avenue — a long, narrow street, squeezed between tall buildings.

My companion and I began to converse, cautiously at first but then with greater confidence. The gendarme escorting us maintained an indulgent attitude. My comrade in misfortune, who had been arrested at the same time as I had, during the previous night, was Boris Nikolayevich Knipovich, son of a professor of zoology. His aunt, Lidiya Mikhailovna Knipovich, known in our Party as 'Dyadenka' (Uncle), had a rich revolutionary past: a record of many years of exile and imprisonment was inevitably included in her colourful biography. Boris Nikolayevich himself was at that time a student in the law faculty of Petersburg University and a member of the Bolshevik group: he particularly studied the agrarian question and had recently produced a small book on the class stratification of Russia's peasantry.

Knipovich, a serious person, made a very agreeable impression on me. Later on we became friends, and I used to visit his family's cosy professorial flat in Gatchinskaya Street, where Nikolai Mikhailovich's wife, Apollinariya Ivanovna, dispensed tea with a kind smile, and silver-haired Nikolai Mikhailovich listened attentively and sympathetically to our political discussions.* Boris Nikolayevich and I always found it amusing that our friendship had begun in a political-police vehicle, when we were being transferred to Spassky police-station. We were both given, by administrative decision, one and the same sentence, exile for three years to Archangel province, but through petitioning by our relatives this was changed to banishment abroad. Having been arrested on that same ill-starred night, May 21-22 1912, we were released from custody for a brief farewell meeting with our families on the same autumn day, October 5.

---

* N.M. Knipovich had himself been in trouble with the police in his youth, when he was expelled from Petersburg University for 'political unreliability'.

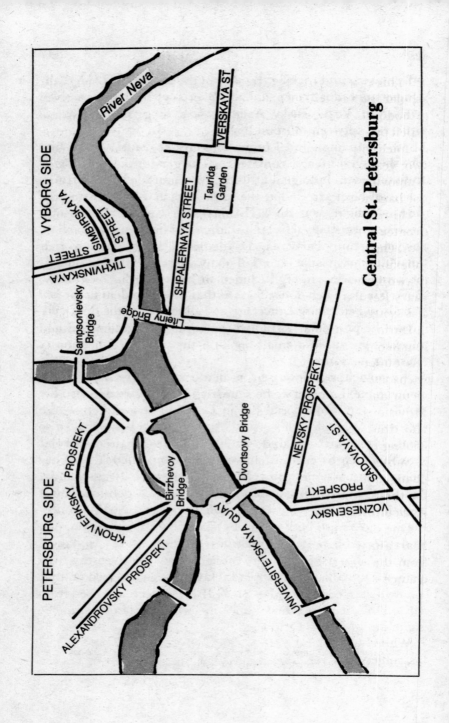

Central St. Petersburg

In his cast of character Boris Nikolayevich was an armchair scholar rather than a practical politician. He was not an orthodox Marxist, and so could not become a Leninist. When he left prison he went to Germany and entered the University of Munich, but he was allowed to study abroad for no more than two years. In July 1914 the imperialist war began, and Knipovich, along with other Russians, was interned, and later got back to Russia.

He returned to Petrograd a furious defencist. Sometimes, over tea in the flat in Gatchinskaya Street, I would grapple with him, engaging in heated debate. But Boris Nikolayevich was inflexible, and quite unwilling to agree with my arguments, drawn from the arsenal of Lenin's *Sotsial-Demokrat*. The February Revolution poured fresh blood into the veins of his defencist system.

During the early days of the February Revolution I ran into him in one of the innumerable corridors of the Taurida Palace. His outlook did not differ in the slightest from that of the Menshevik Tsereteli. He spoke warmly in favour of war to a victorious conclusion, and of wholehearted support for the Provisional Government. We could find no common language, and drew still further apart. Political differences entailed a cooling of our personal relations. We did not meet again.

Subsequently, after the October Revolution, Knipovich changed his views, left the camp of Menshevism, and worked for the Soviet Government, in the People's Commissariat of Agriculture.

One day, while bathing at Yalta, in the Crimea, he had a heart attack. Soon afterwards his cold, lifeless corpse was taken from the water. Boris Nikolayevich died young, and had no chance to develop all the creative gifts he possessed.

IV

While I was talking with Boris Nikolayevich and listening to his conjectures and suggestions that the reason for his arrest was probably the publication of his little book on social-class differentiation among the peasantry, our jarring, broken-down carriage was slowly making its way over the uneven cobbled road-surface towards its destination.

When it reached Sadovaya Street, the carriage turned right and at once entered the yard of a yellow building equipped with a fireman's watchtower.* This was Spassky police station, a intermediate stage in our wanderings from prison to prison.

We were taken into the office, which was on the ground floor. Just as the porter in the lobby of a hotel distributes newly-arrived guests among the vacant rooms in the hotel, so the policeman in the office behind a wooden partition, after checking the information he needed from a thick, tattered book, immediately assigned us our accommodation in this lock-up. Knipovich was put in one cell, I in another. I was not alone, though. The cell to which I was sent was already occupied by a short, stout man with close-cropped dark hair and thick, rather lengthy black moustaches. This was a young Georgian named Machabeli, a machine-feeder in a small, privately-owned printing works. He had been arrested on a denunciation by his employer for involvement in an economic strike. Wooden bunks as black as soot constituted the only furniture of the cell. There was a narrow, barred window in the thick brick wall, right up under the ceiling. The cell was on the first floor and the window looked out on to the yard. However, in order to see through the window and survey the cheerless, miserable yard, laid with cobblestones, we had to stand on our bunks, like the prisoner in Yaroshenko's well-known painting.†

Permanent twilight reigned in the cell. Even when sun-beams, with the motes that played in them, managed to penetrate the cell, they lit up only a small rectangle of the bunks or the floor, while all the other corners remained in twilight.

---

* In Russian towns where there were many wooden buildings and danger from fire was serious, watchtowers were set up and kept manned so that immediate warning could be given of the outbreak of a fire.

† N.A. Yaroshenko's painting 'The Prisoner' (1878) is in the Tretyakov Gallery.

Machabeli, who felt that he was the host in the cell, hospitably offered me tea, and I accepted his offer. Grasping a big nickel-plated teapot with both hands, he poured some strong tea into a tin mug, and held out to me a brown paper bag containing big, white pieces of chipped sugar. I took the first piece to hand. In its hardness and its shape this reminded me of a rock fallen from a cliff, and with an effort, straining my jaws, I began crunching this rock of sugar between my firm young teeth, washing down the fragments with mouthfuls of black, well-brewed tea that smelt like hay. Machabeli started telling about himself at great length, in his pleasant accent. His printing works was somewhere near Blagoveshchenskaya Square. There were not many workers, but this made it all the easier for the boss to exploit them as much as he wanted. Eventually the workers could stand it no longer and demanded a rise in wages and a reduction in their stupefying work-day. For the first time in the history of this 'estate' belonging to a despotic master, an economic strike was declared. The employer had close connections with the police, including the political police. He went to the latter's headquarters and demanded that Machabeli be arrested as the 'ringleader'. The political police at once satisfied the capitalist's demand.

Machabeli was now patiently waiting to be sent off into exile, under guard, and, stroking his round, close-cropped head, was pondering where to be sent, if the choice of locality for his exile should be left to him.

The cells of Spassky police station were crowded with workers and students. There were no close-stools in the cells. From time to time the whole building would echo with the shout: 'Orderly! Orderly!' In response to this call, prolonged and persistent, by a prisoner, the policeman on duty would, after waiting for a few minutes, walk sluggishly to the door of the cell, search long and lazily from among his huge, heavily-rattling bunch of keys for the one he needed, slowly open the door and at last conduct the prisoner, burning with impatience, to the toilet at the end of the corridor.

There he would wait calmly, and then escort the prisoner back to his cell. Sometimes he would grumble that he was being disturbed too often. Now and then he would curse and threaten to refuse to open the cell doors again.

In the evening, before sunset, when the slanting sunbeams that came through the bars seemed to be bidding goodnight to the prisoners, I too went to the door and, applying my lips to the small round aperture, shouted loudly several times: 'Orderly! Orderly! Orderly!'

When I was walking along the corridor, all of a sudden somebody addressed me by name. I turned round. The inspection-hole of the nearest cell-door had no glass in it. Thrust out through it were a pair of plump pink lips: the mouth had a tooth missing. I recognised the voice as that of the student Volodya Gorodetsky, a comrade of my brother's. He had been an inmate of Spassky police-station for several days already, knew the local customs, and in his capacity as an old resident proved helpful to me.

Soon it was dark and time for sleep. Machabeli and I lay down on our broad bunks. But that night I spent a long time turning from side to side and could not get to sleep. The cells in Spassky police station swarmed with fleas and bedbugs.

Prisoners in these cells were not allowed visits, but they could receive food parcels. Standing on the wooden bunks we often saw our relatives, carrying bundles, waiting patiently at the station door for the hour appointed for delivery of these gifts. The library of the lock-up was extremely wretched, consisting of lives of the saints and similar works with a 'soul-saving' content.

It was while I was staying in the building with the watch-tower that I had my first experience of a prison riot. There were a number of workers in Spassky police-station who had been languishing there for a long time without any charge being brought against them, as was required by law. Indignant at this treatment of our comrades, we decided to organise a demonstration of protest. One fine day we began, by concerted agreement, to kick the doors of our cells, to violently cast our tin plates on the floor, and to howl frenziedly: 'Prosecutor! Prosecutor!' The prison trembled.

The noise was heard in Sadovaya Street. All the police guard turned out. The prosecutor was summoned by telephone. The improvised riot stopped. Not long after, the prosecutor arrived. Our protest made the political police dispose of their prisoners more quickly. Those workers against whom no charge was brought were banished from the capital for several years by arbitrary administrative decision. The other unruly rioters were hastily transferred to a prison. One day I was ordered to report at the office with my belongings, taken into the yard, placed in a rickety old carriage, and conveyed to Shpalernaya Street, to the pre-trial detention centre, known as 'DPZ'.

V

After the gloomy and bug-ridden Spassky police-station my one-man cell in the pre-trial detention centre seemed to me like a quite pleasant cheap room in a decayed hotel of the second class. The cell was on the third floor. To the right an iron table was screwed to the wall, and there was a small rectangular bench, also of iron. Beside the table there were shelves on the wall, for books and crockery. To the left stood a cot, covered with a grey blanket made of rough, prickly wool. Alongside the washbasin tap a battered tin mug and a clean towel hung on a long nail. The walls were painted with grey oil-paint.

By the window, instead of a primitive close-stool, a water-closet projected from the wall. As though proud of this achievement of technology, the warder who showed me into the cell pulled the handle and flushed the toilet.

By the door a round push-button was let into the wall. The warder pressed it, the button sank into the wall, and an abrupt metallic sound was heard. 'That's for when you want to call a warder,' my Virgil explained.* In this case the technology was deliberately primitive. An electric bell would have allowed prisoners to remind the authorities of their presence whenever they chose, whereas the long metal rod, striking on the round bowl of a bell, rang briefly and once only, and could function again only when the warder had re-set it.

When the warder left, locking the door behind him, I jumped with both feet on to the WC and looked out of the high barred window. It gave on to the prison yard. In every direction I could see there were high, gloomy walls. Like the honeycombs in a beehive, they were holed with the tiny apertures of cell windows, all covered from outside with stout iron bars. In the middle of the spacious yard, in which some stunted grass pushed up here and there, were the small triangular sections, enclosed by gratings, which were destined for the isolated exercise of the inmates of the one-man cells.

In the centre of these secluded corners, high up under the round wooden roof, a sentry patrolled day and night with a loaded rifle in his hands.

The official prison fare was poor and monotonous. For payment, however, one was permitted to order better-quality food from the cookhouse. These 'private' meals fell into two categories: the 25-kopeck one and the 45-kopeck one. The quality, of course, corresponded to the price. Compared with the official meals they were quite tasty, although the cabbage-soup always had an unbearably excessive amount of pepper in it, enough to burn one's mouth painfully.

As I had been arrested while acting as secretary to the editors of *Pravda*, I was entitled, under our Party rules, to one-half of my wages. Once a month my mother went to the *Pravda* office and collected on my behalf 15 roubles, which was 50 per cent of my wages as editorial secretary. This money was sufficient for me to supplement the official fare.

---

* Raskolnikov ironically compares the warder to the poet Virgil who guides Dante through Hell in the latter's *Divine Comedy*.

As regards spiritual sustenance, however, the situation was much better. True, we were not allowed to read newspapers at all, and only past years' issues of magazines were permitted. On the other hand, the DPZ had a good library. The very first day I was there I obtained the catalogue, and wrote down everything I found in it that I wanted.

During my imprisonment I read a whole heap of books which had been published in old 'thick' journals.* Having acquired some note-books 'numbered and stamped' by the prison administration, I entered in them all the passages that interested me in the works I read. By the end of my stay in prison I had filled several such note-books, which I have preserved to this day.

VI

Every day we were taken out for fifteen minutes' exercise. This was supervised by an old warder with a long grey beard, rounded into the shape of a broad spade, and wearing a warder's cap which he never took off. His heroic chest was densely covered, from shoulder to shoulder, with silver medals that looked like roubles and 50-kopeck pieces. The largest medal was flaunted at his neck. The military bearing which he had retained into old age marked him as a former sergeant-major, or at least a former NCO. Out of respect for his grey hairs, his age and his medals, the other warders always politely addressed him as 'Aleksei Ivanovich'.† This callous, impassive, inscrutable old man, grown hard in military and prison service, regarded it as beneath his dignity to joke or chat with prioners. No smile ever played across his stern face, pale and immobile as a plaster death-mask. Inward mirth found expression with him in a slight tremor of his wrinkles, spreading in

---

* Serious journals which contained weighty articles on non-fiction subjects as well as fiction were known as 'thick' journals.

† It is polite form to address someone by his first name and patronymic. Raskolnikov recalls this warder in *Kronstadt and Petrograd*, when comparing his prison experience in 1917 with that in 1912 (p.216).

rays across his aged, bearded face. Silent and reserved, the old
man personally let the prisoners out into the yard and personally conducted them back to their cells. Our exercise took
place in narrow, triangular kennels that were like horse-boxes,
enclosed on two sides by high wooden fences and on the third
by a wooden grating.

It was possible to observe, through the close-set bars of this
grating, the extremely monotonous life of the prison yard. Here
were two elderly criminal prisoners, dressed in baggy, dirty,
once-white prison uniform, ragged from too much wear, lugging to the rubbish pit a big bucket full of potato peelings, offal
and other kitchen refuse: the bucket gave off a sharp, sour
smell. Over there was a warder in his black jacket, walking
slowly like a well-fed duck on a farm, idly rolling from side to
side as he moved at leisure round the yard, to the accompaniment of the rattling of the huge bunch of keys he carried,
fixed to a massive iron ring.

Our exercise period in the prison yard always passed
quickly. Hardly had we managed to sit down on the bench that
stood in our wooden stall than the warder would suddenly
appear, to drive us back once more under the stone vaults of the
half-dark cells, which after our exercise smelt even worse of the
stuffy prison fumes. Though there was no ventilation panel,
there was a narrow chink in the window-sash which admitted a
thin stream of air: but this was not enough to freshen and
ventilate the damp mustiness that had been accumulating for
decades.

VII

We were allowed two meetings a week with our closest
relatives, on Tuesdays and Fridays. They fetched us from our
cells and led us down to the ground floor by an iron stairway,
which rang loudly from our footsteps. Here we were put for the
time being in an empty room. Sometimes the warder would
close the door, but sometimes, to our great satisfaction, he

would leave it ajar. Then we were summoned in turn, our surnames being called out, to go and meet our visitors. It was in this way that I heard for the first time in prison some familiar names. I learnt that along with me the DPZ held Yevgeny Peters, a tall technology student, who always went about in a long black cloak: he worked in our Bolshevik organisation and had visited me in my flat. Also present was Sergei Dianin, son of a professor at the Army Medical Academy, a slim, long-haired student with the face of an inspired ascetic, who had by chance joined the Anarchists and who was a talented musician; and an expansive university student named Neznamov who later became an Ensign and a Left SR and took part in the October Revolution.*

'Ilyin,' shouted the warder in a cap bearing the sinister letters 'DPZ'. When I heard my name I opened the heavy door, walked along a corridor, over a strip of soft carpeting which muffled my steps, passed the rooms where my comrades were impatiently waiting for their visits to begin, and entered a gloomy, ill-lit room with thick iron bars across the dusty window-pane.

I was followed into the room by a stout, red-faced colonel of gendarmes, walking majestically with his right thumb inside the breast of his ample jacket.† In his left hand he pompously carried a copy of *Novoye Vremya*,§ the large sheets of which trailed lightly across the stone floor. From the lofty height of his portentous dignity, which made him look like a ruffled turkey, he hardly deigned to spare me a passing, profoundly indifferent glance.

My mother hastened into the room, nervously adjusting her drooping pince-nez, which were dulled with tears.

---

* Neznamov accompanied Raskolnikov in his eventful journey from Petrograd to Moscow, shortly after the October Revolution, described in *Kronstadt and Petrograd* (p.324).

† In *Kronstadt and Petrograd* (p.11), the author mentions spotting in the street, soon after the February Revolution, this gendarmerie officer: he had attained the rank of General and was wearing on his chest 'a red bow of colossal size'.

§ *Novoye Vremya* was a newspaper of the extreme Right.

Impetuously, she threw herself on my neck and covered my face with kisses. Small and slight, she made a striking contrast with the corpulent gendarme, who was breathing heavily like someone suffering from asthma.

With a disdainful gesture the colonel showed us where we were to sit — me at the end of the room, my mother on the opposite side of the table, near the door. Spreading his round knees wide, he settled himself down between us on a bentwood chair which creaked under his weight. His stomach rolled over his knees in folds, like jelly, and seemed even bigger than before.

'The meeting lasts ten minutes,' he pronounced in an Olympian tone, and, putting on pince-nez in a thin gold frame, he then buried himself in the unfolded pages of his newspaper.

I began talking with my mother. The colonel of gendarmes, while seeming to read the paper, or else, having put it aside, to be engaged in cleaning his long, carefully trimmed fingernails, listened attentively to our every word. As soon as our conversation approached the subject that most concerned us both, namely, my case, the gendarme, speaking in the harsh, masterful tone of a man used to giving orders, would curtly interrupt us.

'I request you not to talk about that matter,' he said, peremptorily. When, one day, my mother referred to the fact that a rumour was circulating in the city that there was soon to be an amnesty, the gendarme suddenly went purple, and with unexpected agility leapt from his seat, saying sharply: 'That is confidential,' and he threatened to terminate our meeting there and then.

As time went by, we evolved our own 'Aesopian' language.*
When I said 'Go and see Konstantin Stepanovich,' my mother

---

* By 'Aesopian' language is signified language in which what is really meant is only hinted at, by analogy with Aesop's fables, in which stories that have a lesson for human beings are told about animals. Here, Raskolnikov alludes to *Pravda* by using the first name and patronymic (themselves quite common) of Yeremeyev, the paper's managing editor.

understood that I meant: 'Go to the editorial office of *Pravda*.'

Sometimes our meetings were attended by a different gen-darme, who was not so stiff and haughty. When, one day, he heard from my mother that I had been arrested groundlessly, he replied in a condescending way: 'That does happen. The political police sometimes make arrests for absolutely no reason at all.' These liberal words of his revealed the antagonism that existed between the gendarmerie and the political police.

VIII

On the grey wall of my cell, above the table, I found that somebody had written out the prison alphabet. I quickly learnt it off by heart. Communication with one's neighbours by tap-ping provided a great diversion and relieved the burden of loneliness.

Soon I was moved from the third floor to the second, into cell No.111, the three drumsticks, as I jokingly called it. One of the adjoining cells was empty. My neighbour on the other side was a criminal. A family man, he suffered extremely from his imprisonment. 'How they torment us' was what he kept tap-ping out on the wall. Like most of the criminal prisoners, he did not like to recall his past. In the cell above me was a political, the Social-Democrat Alexander Konstantinovich Paykes, with whom I communicated by way of the pipe.

He had been arrested somewhere in the south and brought to the Petersburg DPZ. He told me how the election campaign for the fourth State Duma was going. Although he was not a 'liquidator' but a 'Party man', nevertheless, as a 'conciliator', he was distressed by the fact that the Bolsheviks and Men-sheviks were putting forward separate lists of candidates.

Being a Bolshevik, a 'splitter',* opposed to conciliation, I did not share Comrade Paykes's feelings, but regarded the split

---

* F.F. Ilyin's 'Party name' Raskolnikov is derived from *raskolnik*, a schismatic or 'splitter'. The name goes back to the 'Old-Believer' breakaway from the Russian Orthodox Church in the 17th century.

with the Mensheviks as inevitable and a good thing. After pronouncing the illegal Party dead, the Mensheviks had spat on it as they passed by. In their day-to-day work, they pursued not a revolutionary but a liberal policy in the labour movement, and by their tactics of understanding and accommodation with the Tsarist regime, their trimmed and truncated slogans, they were betraying the revolutionary movement of the proletariat.

One day while I was carrying on a factional discussion with Comrade Paykes via the heating-pipe I was interrupted by the warder on duty, Likharev, a short, bow-legged man, who proceeded to read out to me a long list of ponalties that could be incurred for communication by tapping: deprivation of visits, parcels and exercise periods, no more access to the library, and, finally, confinement in a dark cell.

Books were issued from the prison library every day except Sunday and other holidays. The library was run by a well-built, unusually lively, fair-haired man, whom, though, I hardly ever managed to meet. Only on one occasion did he come to see me in my cell, to rebuke me when, through a moment's carelessness, I had spilled ink over a library book. Exchange of books was always carried out through the warders.

I became good at reading a book a day. In the morning I would hand over the book I had finished, placing in it a slip of paper listing the books and issues of journals I wanted to read, copied out from the big catalogue, and after lunch I would receive a fresh book.

Besides back numbers of 'thick' journals I read the classics and also earnestly applied myself to learned works on social questions. Amongst others, I perused with interest V.I. Semyovsky's *The Peasant Question in the Reign of Catherine II.** This large, two-volume work was, of course, one that I did not read in a single day.

Once I noticed in a book I was reading some lines that were spotted with underscorings and dots. I began to put together

---

* Semyovsky's book had been published in 1881 and 1901.

the letters that were indicated by means of these mysterious marks. They formed words, and these words formed a message. In its time, this had been a warning, brief but grim, that Ivanov was a *provocateur* and Sidorov a cowardly traitor.

On another occasion I deciphered with delight a long message composed in this way by a member of the Social Democratic group in the Second State Duma,* Sergei Nikolayevich Saltykov, describing what had happened during the trial of the Social-Democrat members of that Duma. In this way a link was forged between generations.

IX

One fine day they sent for me, to be interrogated. At noon, soon after lunch had been brought, the staid Alexei Ivanovich came into my cell and, stroking his long grey beard, said in his emotionless voice: 'Please come to the city.'

At first I failed to understand this technical expression. 'Are they going to release me?' was the thought that flashed through my mind. I rushed to the shelf and, with hands trembling from joy, began to assemble my books, soap and toothbrush.

'Without your things,' said the warder, drily, giving me a disapproving look from his unfriendly eyes, a silent rebuke for my slow-wittedness.

I put my things down, walked out of the cell, and began dejectedly descending the iron stairs. The warder followed close behind me.

Two strapping gendarmes were waiting for me in the prison office. They wrote something in a big, solidly-bound book that lay there, and then, drawing their swords, escorted me into the yard.

The sun was shining brightly, festively. One gendarme walked ahead of me and the other behind. The sharp blades of their long, straight swords gleamed blindingly in the sunlight.

---

* The Second State Duma was dissolved by the Tsar on June 3, 1907, after the entire Social-Democratic fraction had been arrested on a trumped-up charge of conspiracy.

In the yard, which was paved with large, uneven cobble-stones, they put me into an old carriage, half falling to pieces, to which a pair of bony, underfed horses were harnessed. One of the gendarmes clambered in awkwardly and plumped down beside me, while the other took the front seat, facing us. The horses set off and, rumbling noisily over the uneven stones, threatening at every moment to overturn, the carriage slowly began its journey. The horses' hooves resounded from the cobbled roadway.

It was a bright, sunny day, and as hot as midsummer. The blue blind, though lowered, did not completely cover the window of the carriage, and when it shook I was able to observe a little corner of the outside world. Never before had it seemed to me so attractive and lovable. After the damp cell even the warm stuffiness of the carriage was pleasant to me. I gazed with delight, through the gap left by the blind, at the street we were traversing. The gendarme who was sitting opposite me noticed this and, giving me a hostile look, quickly drew the curtain. I shifted my gaze to my companions. They sat in silence, their legs wide apart. Those legs were tightly encased in blue riding-breeches and polished top-boots. They rested their hands, which were abnormally large, upon the black leather scabbards of their swords. Their stupid faces, moist and flushed with the heat, betrayed not the slightest glimmer of thought. Their strong, healthy bodies gave off an unbearable smell of sweat, sharp and sour.

Profiting by a moment when my companions were talking together, I furtively moved the blind aside and looked out of the window. We were passing the Taurida Garden. The dense green vegetation threw a patterned chiaroscuro on to its broad avenues, crackling with gravel, which were filled with a cheer-ful, noisy crowd. I wanted terribly to be out there mingling with these strollers. 'What happiness it is to be free,' I thought. Only when in prison, deprived of freedom, does one learn to value freedom properly. When I was free I failed completely to appreciate my good fortune — I did not even notice it.

My thoughts were interrupted by a sudden jolt. The carriage had stopped. Some gates were opened, with a piercing squeal, and our old wagon, which was on the point of disintegrating, creaked into the yard of a white, two-storey building in Tverskaya Street. This was the headquarters of the gendarmerie.

Along narrow, dirty corridors I was conducted to the room which served as a waiting-room. Its only furniture was a plain wooden stool, absurdly set down in the middle of the floor. Diagonally across the painted flooboards a worn strip of carpet was laid, and, feeling tense at the prospect of interrogation, I began walking to and fro along it. The window of the room looked out on a green garden, where thick grass grew and there were young apple-trees with spreading branches.

I did not have long to wait. After a few minutes the door opened with a squeak, and an NCO led me into the office of Colonel of Gendarmerie Pokroshinsky. Tall, stoutly-built and puffy-faced, with cheeks that drooped like a bulldog's, with big blue bags under his sharp black eyes, and with dashingly upward-twisted and well-dyed moustaches, he slowly rose from his chair behind a desk, his silver spurs jingling, squared his broad shoulders, and with a dignified air offered me his hand, saying, with exaggerated politeness: 'Please be so good as to sit down, Mr Ilyin.' Without replying, I sat down on the chair assigned to me.

'Do you smoke? Would you like a cigarette?' And, with a sweeping, histrionic gesture, Pokroshinsky proffered me his massive silver cigarette case. I thanked him and declined.

'You are charged under Article 102, with belonging to the Russian Democratic [sic] Workers' Party,' said Pokroshinsky, in an icy tone and immediately assuming a serious, businesslike manner. 'Do you plead guilty?'

'No,' I replied, without batting an eyelid.

'Write it down,' said the gendarme, handing me a sheet of paper.

Then he opened a locked drawer in his desk and pulled out a

Tsarist police searching for revolutionary literature

big packet of letters, papers and manuscripts. I realised that this was the correspondence that had been removed from my flat when it was searched.

Certain lines in the letters had been underscored and there were marks in the margins, made with blue pencil.

'What can you tell me about this communication? Who wrote it?' the gendarme demanded sternly, and fixed his disagreeable goggle-eyes upon me.

Before me lay a postcard signed 'Leonid.' I remained silent.

'From whom did you receive it?' Pokroshinsky insistently repeated his question.

'I don't remember,' I said, after a short pause.

'Well, you know,' protested the gendarmerie officer, putting his hands in his pockets and leaning back in his chair, 'you're not a child. Who is going to believe that you don't remember the name of the writer of that postcard, though he addressed you in the familiar manner and is on friendly terms with you? Keep in mind, Mr Ilyin, the fact that every denial on your part will only worsen your fate.'

He fell silent and stared straight at me with his evil, gleaming black eyes.

'So, then, perhaps you do remember, after all?' he added, giving ironical emphasis to each word.

'No, I don't remember,' I repeated, with blunt stubbornness. I realised that my answer was unconvincing, but what I was doing was fully justified by my unwillingness to betray a comrade.

'Very well, then. It will be the worse for you,' said the gendarme, spitefully. He was angry at the failure of his attempt to discover the writer of that postcard.

I shrugged my shoulders silently.

With a worried air, Pokroshinsky rummaged in the desk-drawer, in which papers lay in disorder, and at last extracted and triumphantly laid before me on the desk a letter written on a quarter-sheet of semi-transparent foreign paper, in a neat, round hand.

This was a letter from Maxim Gorky, sent to me from Capri, which I had preserved in my archives like a precious relic.

In my capacity as librarian of the Petersburgers' Society at the Polytechnical Institute I had written to Gorky to ask him to let us have some of the publications of the 'Znanie' press for our library. Gorky readily responded to my request and at once wrote back to me courteously agreeing to our receiving the books we wanted. He gave his letter, which was sent at a time when student strikes and demonstrations were in full swing, this political conclusion: 'With all my heart I wish you courage in the difficult days you are now living through. Russia will not rise again until we Russians learn to stand up for our human dignity and fight for the right to live as we want.' The letter was signed: A. Peshkov.*

The concluding lines of the letter had been underscored by the gendarme's blue pencil.

'A letter from the well-known émigré writer Maxim Gorky was found among your papers. Do you know him personally?' asked Pokroshinsky, now resuming a more polite tone.

I replied in the negative.

'And what is the meaning of this expression: "fight for the right to live as we want"?'

I again pleaded ignorance, and said that this question should be addressed to Gorky.

The gendarme fidgeted irritatedly in his chair, and was on the point of uttering something harsh, but restrained himself. He pulled out of the drawer my own writings and the editorial papers which had been removed when my flat was searched.

'Who is this Raskolnikov?' he demanded venomously, drawling the words with an air of triumph.

'I really don't know,' I repeated, giving the same considered reply, in a dreary monotone.

'Isn't that your own pseudonym as a writer?' he asked,

* Raskolnikov recalls this letter in connection with his personal encounter with Gorky in 1917, in *Kronstadt and Petrograd* (p.57).

mistakenly stressing the second syllable in 'pseudonym'.

Seeing that he would get nothing out of me, he asked me to sign my name and terminated the interrogation.

I looked out of the window. Tverskaya Street was deserted, and looked like a street in a provincial town. Unimpressive white buildings gleamed in the sunlight. They led me out into the yard, and in the same old-fashioned carriage returned me to the pre-trial detention centre.

X

A few weeks later I was summoned for a second interrogation. This concluded the investigation by the gendarmerie. From the jurisdiction of the gendarmerie's authority of the province I was transferred to that of the Special Board attached to the office of the Governor of Petersburg. By decision of this organ I was condemned to three years' exile in Archangel province. At my mother's request my exile to the North was commuted to banishment abroad. On October 5, a dark, rainy day, at a time when the street-lamps had already been lit, I was released from custody. At the door of the pre-trial detention centre I again bumped into Knipovich, who had been released that same day. Seated in a cab and clutching with both hands the big bundle containing my things and my books, I feasted my eyes on the Neva as we crossed the Liteiny Bridge, and joyfully inhaled the fresh, cool, air, which was already touched a little by the dank humidity of autumn. I was soon back in my room on the Vyborg Side. They had allowed me three days for saying goodbye to my family. This time passed quickly, imperceptibly, like the flying clouds in the sky on a clear, windy day.

During this period I was, of course, very earnestly shadowed. Detectives hastened both before me and behind me. The ones in front kept twisting their heads to one side so as, without actually turning round, to keep me in view out of the corners of their eyes. At nearly every turning in the Nevsky Prospekt they were changed, and responsibility for me was handed over to another pair of sleuths.

This surveillance was so thorough that, one day, when I left home intending to take a packet of papers to one of my comrades, but found the detectives dogging my heels, I felt obliged to go back indoors for no obvious reason, lest I compromise my comrade.

All the same, I did manage to get to the editorial office of *Pravda*. The little rooms were smoke-filled and stuffy. Acting as secretary in place of me was my comrade in the Bolshevik group in the Polytechnic Institute, Vyacheslav Mikhailovich Molotov (Skryabin).*

'So, then, you are now going to become one of our "comrades abroad",' he said with a smile, rubbing his close-cropped dark head as he gave me a firm handshake.

I intended to go to Paris, having chosen that city because Comrade Lenin lived there and it was where our Bolshevik Central Committee was located. However at the editorial office of *Pravda*, Konstantin Stepanovich Yeremeyev, smacking his lips with satisfaction and without removing from his mouth the pipe he was smoking, informed me that Vladimir Ilyich had already moved from Paris to Galicia.†

'Why not send him to where he'll be under the high authority of Ilyich?' suggested Stepan Stepanovich Danilov, looking up from a manuscript and tugging nervously at his pointed beard, which made his face look longer and so emphasised still more sharply the leanness of his cheeks, hollowed by illness.

'No, that's not worth while,' phlegmatically objected Nikolai Guryevich Poletayev, looking round at everyone from under his brows. 'It would be hard for him to find work in Galicia. Better send him to Paris.'

Konstantin Stepanovich picked up a pencil, drew me a plan of the Latin Quarter, which was where the poorer émigrés

---

* Skryabin was Molotov's real name: he was a nephew of the well-known composer whose name is usually spelt, in the West, in the French form, as 'Scriabine'.

† Lenin moved to Galicia (Austrian Poland) at the end of June 1912, and stayed there until the outbreak of war in 1914. He lived in Cracow during the winter and in the village of Poronino in the summer.

Yeremeyev

Molotov

huddled, and gave me a number of addresses of Bolsheviks resident in Paris. This plan was found on me when I was arrested at Insterburg,* and provided the gendarmes of East Prussia with an excuse for suspecting that I was a spy. Fortunately, Konstantin Stepanovich had written the names of the streets on his plan, and this saved me.

That same day at the *Pravda* office I made the acquaintance of Comrade Sergeyev, a small, hunchbacked man.† 'Aren't you Sergeyev-Tsensky?' I asked. 'No, not Sergeyev-Tsensky,' he replied, with a smile on his full, protruding lips. He was a former émigré and also supplied me with some addresses. He warned me that without knowing the French language it was difficult to find work, and told how he had walked all over France and Italy in search of casual, temporary employment.

After warm farewells to all the 'Pravdists', in the evening of October 9, in a green third-class carriage, which shook disagreeably on its crude springs and lurched when there were abrupt jerks, I hastened towards the Russo-German frontier, to the steady and unwelcome accompaniment of autumn rain, monotonously and despondently beating down on the iron roof of my carriage.

---

* Now Chernyakhovsk.

† It is not clear who this Sergeyev was. F.A. Sergeyev (Artyom), 1883-1921, had been an émigré in Paris in 1902, but in 1912 he was in Australia. There was also A.V. Sergeyev (Petrov), 1893-1933, who joined the Party in 1911. S.N. Sergeyev-Tsensky, 1875-1958, was a well-known novelist: one of his works, *Brusilov's Breakthrough*, came out in English translation in 1945.

Fraternisation
A story

In a wide clearing overgrown with short, lush grass, behind wooden chevaux-de-frise intertwined with rusty barbed wire, in deep trenches that smelt of wet earth, a group of soldiers sat, in awkward, twisted poses, drinking their morning tea. It was stifling in the close atmosphere of the damp, dark dug-out and the soldiers had taken their tin mugs filled with steaming tea out into the open air. Not far from them, beside a stinking yellow puddle, stood a pyramid of shabby, scratched Japanese rifles with flat-bladed, dagger-like bayonets which resembled long kitchen-knives. The baggy, faded jackets the soldiers wore were belted not with leather straps, as at the beginning of the war, but with thin strips of canvas. They were shod in clumsy, down-at-heel boots. Their calves were carelessly wrapped in greenish puttees. Beside them, in the dug-out, on the dark bunks and the damp earthen floor lay their knapsacks of grey bag-canvas, their mess-tins of thin tinplate, and their mis-shapen padded jackets, in which the wadding was of raw tow. Previously their knapsacks had been made of tarpaulin-canvas and their mess-tins of copper, and the wadding in their jackets had been cotton-wool, but the long-drawn-out war had changed all that.

Because it was Easter, the soldiers had been issued with butter, and they were calmly and in businesslike fashion spreading this on their bread. Every slice they covered on both sides with a thick layer of yellow, salted butter.

'Well, if they've given us butter, we're certainly going to

retreat,' said Shapilkin, swallowing bits of black bread unchewed and appreciatively sucking his fingers, which glistened with butter. He was a swarthy, elderly man from the reserve, with a black, tangled beard and thick, tousled hair. 'When, not long ago, I was on the Bzura, near Warsaw, that was always a sign for us: if they issued butter, that meant, get ready, grease the soles of your boots, we're soon going to do a bunk.'* His dark, sunken eyes with blue whites twinkled sarcastically under his beetling brows.

'Gypsy, you waggle your tongue like a cow waggles its tail,' replied in a calm voice a grey-moustached soldier named Tabakov, who had recently joined the Bolshevik Party. Before the war he had worked as a milling-machine operator in the Aivaz factory.† Shapilkin, nicknamed Gypsy, made a wry face and looked at Tabakov malevolently, but made no rejoinder. Blue-eyed Zhivets, a strapping young fellow with a face that was as red as if he had been scalded, reached out awkwardly for the tin tea-pot and, making splashes, poured himself a mug of hot tea.

'How sick I am of these damned lentils,' he said, his thin, uncertain alto slightly drawling the words. 'They used to feed the stuff to horses, and they said it made their hair fall out, but now they give it to human beings to eat as well. We only get little bits of meat, and then it's uneatable, smells like carrion. I'm not going to eat anything more, only drink tea.'

'There's precious little bread, the meat stinks, the fish is rotten, and we get no more than a miserable allowance of sugar,' interjected Shapilkin, as he carelessly splashed his tea-leaves on to the grass. 'I expect the pot-bellies have enough, but there's none for us. Neither tobacco, nor soap, nor uniforms — nothing. And they pay us 75 kopecks a month. Well, to the devil with them.'

And, enraged, he began rolling a cigarette, using a fragment

---

* The Russians had been forced to retreat from the area Shapilkin mentions in 1915.
† The Aivaz factory was one of the principal factories in Petersburg.

of newspaper. Zhivets fell into a reverie. He remembered his native village, the low, ramshackle hut with the roof of dirty straw and the dark windows and he remembered, too, his old mother, with her kind, wrinkled face and grey, sorrowful eyes. Wearing her red headscarf tied high, she kneaded the resilient dough and with a long shovel placed the round loaves of rye-bread in the oven. On Saturdays, after giving her family their meal, she took her shoes off and, with her skirt tucked up, her face flushed and wet with sweat, stooped low and, standing with her bare legs, with their muscular calves, placed wide apart, she washed the dirty wooden floor, through the big cracks in which blew, as from a cellar, thin currents of damp, cold air.

'I wanted very badly not to go to the war,' said Zhivets, meditatively, changing the subject of the conversation to what most worried and tormented him. 'We're settlers. We had only just started up our home, built a hut, bought a cow, reared some poultry, when, bang, the war came. Soon they were calling up our lads ... Well, they took me, too. I got very frightened! I really didn't want to go to the war.'

'Who did?' observed Shapilkin, gloomily, as he continued to smoke the big cigarette he had rolled for himself, and stretched out at full length his legs in their rough, broad-toed boots, bespattered with thick, sticky mud.

'Ye-e-s ... I was terribly upset,' blue-eyed Zhivets went on, forgetting the mug of tea he had poured out for himself. 'I remember it as though it was today ... On the last night I went out into the yard. It was so quiet ... Nothing stirred. The cow was lying on straw in the shed: she mooed ... The horses were munching their hay. Little stars shone in the blue sky. It was just paradise, that's what it was ... And now I had to go to the war, to shed my blood for I didn't know what ... Why do people fight? There's plenty of land. You'd think there was enough for everyone ... I walked all round the yard. The chicks were calling to each other in wheezy voices. It was so hard for me to leave my own home. My heart really ached.'

'All the same, you're going to fight, Zhivets,' said Shapilkin, smoking his cigarette and puffing out a blue-grey cloud of stinking *makhorka* smoke. 'They say in the papers that Kerensky has declared for war until complete victory.'

'In *Okopnaya Pravda** they say,' Tabakov broke in excitedly, 'that a British minister has declared, straight out: "We'll fight to the last drop of blood of a Russian soldier" . . . Not a British soldier, a Russian soldier . . . That's what he said. Word of honour. We're so much cannon fodder to stop up gaps with. What fine allies they are . . .'

'Last year, when they were in trouble,' said Shapilkin, wiping his moustache with the back of his hand, 'we had to take the offensive. What a lot of men were done for, what a lot of orphans, widows and cripples were made.† And now nobody can see when it will end. They chatter about peace, but it's only chatter.'

'But how good it would be to have peace and get back home soon,' said Zhivets dreamily, taking off his crumpled cap and passing his hand over his round, tow-haired, close-cropped head. 'The people have now become like brothers . . . Only the war oppresses us . . . We've been shedding our blood for three years — how easy it is to say that . . . And when will this slaughter of us wretched people be ended? After all, these are our brothers. They've done no wrong. They don't owe us anything. Why should we fight them?'

'The devil only knows what they mean to do with us. We won't attack, anyway,' said Shapilkin, firmly, and in his irritation he hit out at the crumbling wall of the trench.

'We mustn't attack, we must fraternise,' explained Tabakov loudly, his grey eyes suddenly sparkling. 'Comrade Lenin says—'

'Down with Lenin!' came a voice from the dug-out. 'He came from Wilhelm. In a sealed train . . .'

---

* *Okopnaya Pravda* (Trench Truth) was the Bolshevik soldiers' newspaper. It began to appear on April 30 (May 13) 1917.

† In March 1916 the Russians launched an offensive in order to relieve the pressure on Verdun. In a single fortnight they lost 150,000 men.

'The Bolsheviks are splendid people,' shouted Tabakov, waving his arms. 'Especially Lenin . . . I heard him speak when I was on leave . . . On the Petersburg Side, from the balcony of Kshesinskaya's house . . .'

'The SRs are better. They're for land and liberty,' broke in a short, puny, black-haired soldier.

'You can't made out which party is best. They've got things in such a mess, it can't be sorted out,' someone rumbled in a deep bass.

'The Bolsheviks are for peace. They're against the war and against the bourgeois,' Tabakov went on, with fervour. 'We are tormented, hungry, cold and in rags, we are rotting in filthy, wet dug-outs, we are being eaten by lice, but the bourgeois in the rear are drinking champagne, rolling around in cars with their mistresses, raking in the money, so they keep on bawling: "War until victory!" But where is it, this victory?'

'It seems the devil has gobbled it up,' muttered Shapilkin gloomily.

There was laughter. Tabakov's warm, sincere words had touched the soldiers' hearts. But the Mensheviks and SRs stubbornly objected to fraternisation, and only the Bolshevik soldiers ardently supported Tabakov. A fierce, passionate argument broke out between them.

'Who can make them out?' a bass voice suddenly droned. 'Perhaps it's true, perhaps the Bolsheviks do mean well.'

'That's right, the Bolsheviks are good people. They are the only ones who tell the truth,' several men contributed.

'They stand for peace,' said a loud voice from the interior of the machine-gun post.

'They're against the bourgeois,' said someone in the dug-out.

'They're the only ones who are for the workers and the peasants.'

'The Bolsheviks are our people,' came from the winding communication trenches.

'So, then, lads, let's fraternise,' cried Tabakov joyfully. 'Let's do as Lenin says and turn the imperialist war into a civil war.

Our Party group has decided to fraternise, comrades!'

'Fine, fine! Down with the war ! Let's fraternise!' came cheerful cries from the whole length of the trench.

'Don't you dare fraternise! It's treason to the fatherland and to the revolution!' shouted the short dark man. Then, seeing that he was helpless to stop it, he hurried away to warn the commanders.

'Let's stop firing and fraternise, and then, you'll see, the war will end,' Zhivets cried with enthusiasm, and ran swiftly into the dug-out. In a minute he was back again, holding a wide red towel which served as a flag on ceremonial occasions, and also a tin plate, on which lay a small white *paskha,** and some gaily painted eggs, purchased in the nearest town.

'We've had enough, Stepa, of shedding our blood for the interests of the capitalists,' said Shapilkin, excitedly, as he slapped Zhivets on the back. 'They came to blows, they took a beating, they made a hell of a mess, and now it's time to stop.'

Speechless with emotion, Zhivets smiled a rapturous smile with his wide mouth. In an instant the soldiers hastened to the entrance of the dug-out. Tabakov took a piece of chalk and, knitting his brows, slowly and with concentration began to inscribe letters two-feet high on the flag. After sticking tall, thin poles in the ground, the soldiers fixed between them the long pieces of red cloth with the inscription Tabakov had made: 'Down with the war! Greetings to the working people of the West!'

The volunteers, officers and NCOs and the Menshevik and SR soldiers got excited, shouted and argued, but none of their arguments could hold the soldiers back from fraternisation, and so they morosely withdrew into the dug-outs to drink coffee.

---

* *Paskha* here means the sweet dish made of curds, butter and raisins, eaten at Easter.

II

The Austrian soldiers in their greyish-green uniforms and crumpled képis rose waist-high out of their trenches, waved little white flags and, comically mispronouncing the Russian words, shouted at the tops of their voices: 'Russian, don't shoot! Make peace!'

'Look, look, the Austrians are coming! More and more of them!' cried the Russian soldiers, excited by this extraordinary spectacle.

'My word, yes, what a lot of them are pouring out of the trenches,' said Shapilkin, amazed, as he gravely stroked his beard.

Zhivets purposefully took out a clean handkerchief, shook it, spread it neatly on the grass, and carefully smoothed it with his palms, rough as a cat's tongue. Then he wrapped in it the white curd *paskha* and three painted eggs. Taking a small white flag and holding it high above his head, his right arm stretched out stiffly, he held the neatly tied bundle in his left hand, taking care not to crush the delicate *paskha*. Then, with difficulty, he climbed over the barbed wire. Nearly all his fingers were soon bleeding from scratches. Four Austrians, in greenish képis with long peaks and small, round, cockades, like buttons, jumped out of their trenches and advanced towards him. Zhivets stopped.

'Come on, come into the middle!' shouted, in Russian, a Czech whose face was grey with dust.

'*Pan*,* I can't cope with four,' Zhivets shouted back in his youthful, ringing voice, and made a gesture of helplessness.

The Austrians consulted together, and three of them went back and sat, with their legs dangling, on the edge of their trench. An Austrian soldier with light-coloured eyebrows moved hesitantly towards Zhivets, clutching his broad belt, with a puzzled smile on his face. When they came alongside each other they both, as though at a command, took off their

* *Pan* is the Czech equivalent of 'Mister'.

caps, flung them on the ground and embraced warmly.

Sweating and emotional, smiling with joy, Zhivets handed the Austrian soldier his present.

'*Danke schön, danke schön,*' said the Austrian, cheerfully nodding, as, flushed, he picked up his képi from the ground and shyly smoothed his fair, dishevelled hair.

'What's your name?' asked Zhivets, unceremoniously prodding the other man in the chest with his forefinger. 'Your name — what?'

'Wurstmacher, Wurstmacher,' the Austrian replied, after a moment's hesitation, and smiled broadly. He sat down on the stump of a recently felled birch-tree, undid the bundle and cordially offered one of the eggs to Zhivets, who, however, shook his head, saying, 'Eat it, I brought it for you, eat it.'

And Wurstmacher began, with unconcealed avidity, to stuff big pieces of the white crumbly *paskha* into his mouth.

When he had eaten his fill and brushed the crumbs off himself, Zhivets took him delicately by the arm and, as though out with a young lady, walked up and down with him at the foot of a hillock which Shapilkin called, in his old Siberian dialect, a *sopka*. Gesticulating in a remarkably lively and expressive way with his dry, thin hand, Zhivets strove to explain something to the Austrian.

Thousands of eyes watched Zhivets and Wurstmacher tensely from both sides. Then, as though at a command, the Russian soldiers, shouting 'Hurrah!', flung themselves, with their bare hands, on the barbed-wire obstacles. In a moment the pickets were uprooted and broken with a crack, and the torn barbed wire lay lifeless on the ground. The Austrian soldiers likewise opened wide gaps through their barbed wire. Then the Russians and Austrians, as though fatigued by the work they had just accomplished, advanced towards each other timidly and cautiously. The sight of the live enemy — he who only yesterday had been firing his rifle at them, spreading death and destruction — struck everyone with unreasoning, terrifying anxiety. As they drew nearer, they came to a halt, staring at this enemy: but when they saw the others' simple, open, peasant faces, the ice broke at once. Like the smashed pickets of the barbed-wire obstacles, in a second the distrust and hatred between them was destroyed — that distrust and hatred which had been instilled into these peaceful ploughmen by their officers and generals so that they might slash, stab and kill each other for the sake of plundering, conquest and profit by greedy landlords, bankers, factory-owners and merchants. The soldiers of both armies rushed impulsively towards each other and, shouting, began to shake hands and embrace. Big, limpid tears poured down the faces of many of them. Not knowing each other's language, they could not converse, but they understood each other very well by instinct and intuition.

'Please be our guests, comrades!' said Tabakov, hospitably, offering a round loaf of black bread and a sugar-loaf wrapped in blue paper.

'Thank you very much for this. We haven't seen any sugar for eight months now,' replied the Austrians, gratefully, and offered the Russians cigars and cigarettes in return.

The remains of the dead from the previous year had not yet been removed from the clearing. As in *Ruslan and Lyudmila*,* it was strewn with dead men's bones. The Austrian soldiers called it 'the valley of death'. Now, the Russians and Austrians collected up the yellowed skulls and bones that were lying about on the grass. They gathered them into a heap which soon grew into a high pyramid, as in Vereshchagin's picture *The Apotheosis of War*.†

Treading hard on his spade, Shapilkin dug a grave. The other soldiers, who had removed their caps and their képis, helped him in solemn silence. Within an hour a broad, deep pit had been dug, and into it were cast the bones and skulls,

---

* In Pushkin's poem *Ruslan and Lyudmila*, on which Glinka based an opera, Ruslan passes, on his way to rescue Lyudmila, through 'the valley of the dead', an ancient battlefield littered with the bones of warriors.

† V.V. Vereshchagin's painting 'The Apotheosis of War', painted in 1871-1872, is in the Tretyakov Gallery.

making a dry rattling sound as they fell. Over the grave, when it
had been filled in, a low rectangular mound was raised. Standing round this hillock the soldiers sang a funeral hymn.

When this ceremony was over, the fair-haired Wurstmacher
produced, for the funeral feast, a bottle of rum with a long neck
and a picture of a smiling, curly-haired Negro on the label, and
slyly began began pouring this rum into glasses. Shapilkin
boldly clinked glasses with him, swallowed his glass of strong
rum in one gulp, grunted, and then appreciatively wiped his
wet lips and moustache with the back of his hand.

All over the clearing groups of Russians and Austrians were
sitting, vying with each other in hospitality, clinking glasses,
talking loudly, smoking, drinking rum and brandy. This narrow clearing, bounded by two rows of barbed wire, looked not
so much like the scene of recent fighting as like that of a picnic
or a popular outing.

'We've thrown off our allegiance to Nicholas. You throw off
your allegiance. That'll be a fair exchange,' cried Shapilkin,
cheerfully waving his swarthy hand.

'That's right, comrade, that's right! Then there will be
peace,' agreed Tabakov, enthusiastically, striking a fist into the
palm of his other hand. The volunteer Poyarkov, a former
student, who had cycled all over Germany before the war, now,
proud of his advantage over the rest of the men, diligently
translated Shapilkin's words into German.

Wurstmacher listened attentively to the translation and,
nervously smoothing his unruly locks, said sincerely and
frankly, with a quiver in his voice: 'Russian . . . You have no
Tsar now. We will soon throw ours off the throne, as well. Let's
make peace . . . We'll be brothers forever . . . In God's name,
don't fire at us, but only into the air . . . And we, too, won't fire
at you.'

Wurstmacher added that they had recently been brought
there from the Italian front and had been ordered to attack, but
had successfully refused.

'Why war? Who needs war? The rich need it, but we don't,'

cried Shapilkin loudly, his dark, deep-set eyes gleaming, as he
pressed against Wurstmacher, who fell back blushing with
embarrassment.

Tabakov, carrying out the decision taken by the Party group,
was gravely and rather solemnly giving a talk about the war.
The Austrian soldiers listened with bated breath and open-
mouthed to Poyarkov's hesitating translation, as to a new,
unheard-of revelation.

'So, then, — will you attack us?' demanded Tabakov, as he
wiped his perspiring brow.

'No, never,' came the firm, convinced reply of the Austrians.

Tabakov hurried back to the trench and returned with a
small, battered camera, with some black calico glued to it.

'We're going to have our photo taken, comrades.' In Russian
and German, the message was passed around the clearing.
Everybody gathered near Tabakov, who, placing his short
strong legs wide apart, was silently and with concentration
setting up his apparatus, as though performing some holy rite.
Some of the men sat down on the grass, with a relaxed air,
others knelt behind them, and those at the very back stood
upright. Many Russians and Austrians put their arms round
each other and smiled happily.

The noon-day sun shone brightly from a high, cloudless sky.
Hungry crows circles, cawing frenziedly, over the green clearing.

'Look, the crows are upset. Obviously, they're protesting
against our fraternisation. They, too, I dare say, would like to
eat,' said Shapilkin in his loud voice.

One of the grinning soldiers could not refrain from chuck-
ling, and others found it hard to keep their smiles from breaking
into laughter. At that very moment the camera clicked, and
then Tabakov, stiff with tension, a blue vein bulging in his
forehead, instantly emerged and let out a sigh of relief. Everyone stirred, moved about and began to cough and chat.

'And now let's show you our dances, and then you show us
yours,' exclaimed Zhivets gaily, in his thin, high voice, choking
with joy.

Guitars and balalaikas were brought from the trenches. Somebody began playing an accordion. Zhivets gave a shout and dashingly started to dance the *gopak*. He squatted, throwing out his thin young legs, then suddenly straightened up and, with arms firmly akimbo, spun round so fast that he seemed to have two faces. At the end of his dance, staggering, breathing hard and wiping the sweat from his red face, which seemed to be on fire, he shyly withdrew.

'Bravo! Bravo!' cried the Austrians, clapping as though in a theatre.

'Now it's your turn,' said Zhivets to Shapilkin, panting and gulping air convulsively, like a fish caught and thrown on the sand.

'All right, then,' replied Shapilkin, defiantly. With a negligent air he put his hands on his hips and slowly, gravely, as though unwilling, he began to dance. To the sound of the *Kamarinskaya* tinkling from a balalaika, he moved with a smile over the grass, stamping his feet and squatting. Suddenly he pulled a dirty handkerchief out of his pocket and, waving this in an affected manner over his shaggy head, he floated round in a circle, ceremoniously, importantly, like a majestic peahen. Fascinated by this unfamiliar dance, the Austrian soldiers followed his every movement with fixed smiles. Suddenly the bearded Shapilkin grabbed a pale, pock-marked Austrian and whirled him into a wild pirouette. Other soldiers, laughing, joined in the round-dance and, happy and carefree as children, they circled again and again on the soft, bright-green, sweet-scented grass.

III

Lanky Prince Windischgrätz belonged to an ancient and distinguished family of the Hungarian aristocracy.* He loved to tell, with pride, how his grandfather, the stern, grey-whiskered Field-Marshal, had in 1848 bombarded Prague and subdued

---

* The Windischgrätz family were not Hungarian, they came from Styria.

Vienna with fire and sword, and in the following year had savagely crushed rebel Hungary.

The fraternisation by the Austrian soldiers, whom he, as a Hungarian magnate, had always regarded with haughty contempt, had filled him with anger and fury. The commander of the Austrian Army, the cunning General Rohr, seeing that this fraternisation could not be dealt with by forcible means, decided to send Windischgrätz, as an experienced spy, into the Russian lines in order to find out what he could about the strength and the morale of the enemy. As passport, he gave him a packet, sealed with red wax, addressed to the headquarters of the Russian Army.

Red-faced, balding, dark-haired, with black, staring eyes, bristling reddish eyebrows and a long, thin neck, Ludwig Windischgrätz crossed the line of the front with anxiously beating heart. He was at once surrounded by a group of Russian soldiers. At the sight of an officer's grey greatcoat the fraternising Austrians had scattered and hidden themselves in the thick, tall bushes.

'I have the honour to present myself — Prince Windischgrätz,' he muttered drily, in German. 'But where are the hostages? Please send them across to our trenches.'

Volunteer Poyarkov, with the particoloured braid on his soldier's shoulder-straps, repeated what Windischgrätz had said, word for word.

'Well, lads, who'll volunteer to go as a hostage?' Tabakov asked the soldiers, who were all gazing at Windischgrätz. His officer's epaulettes, the stars on his high upstanding collar and his entire haughty, important bearing struck them as funny.

'I'll go,' said Zhivets, happy to undertake a worthy and dangerous responsibility for which not everyone would be willing. And, stooping from habit, he ran along the trench: the worn soles of his rust-coloured boots flashed in the air as, swinging his long arms, he leapt awkwardly on to the parapet and trotted across the broad clearing. His tall, thin figure soon vanished into the Austrian trenches.

'Please sit down,' said Tabakov to the Austrian officer.

'Thank you very much,' replied Windischgrätz, settling himself down on a grassy hummock and stretching his long legs in their black, lacquered leggings. With an independent air he unfastened his greatcoat and produced from his jacket pocket a flat silver cigarette-case, on which gleamed an embossed decoration in gold and enamel: a Prince's crown, a patterned monogram, the head of a beautiful woman, a big bottle of champagne, and the brown muzzle of a long-eared Irish setter.

'Please smoke, gentlemen,' he said, addressing the soldiers around him, as he politely offered his cigarette-case, closely packed with short cigarettes which had gold tips instead of the mouthpieces the Russians were used to.

Tabakov declined politely. Some of the others hesitantly reached out for cigarettes.

'How many regiments are fraternising?' asked Windischgrätz, with an innocent air, as he took off his cloth-covered spiked helmet. Big drops of sweat ran down his red face.

'What, as a matter of fact, are you after?' interrupted Tabakov, who was speculating about the enemy's intentions. Poyarkov, stammering slightly, translated Tabakov's question, deliberately omitting the words 'as a matter of fact'. To his surprise, he could not remember the German equivalent of that expression.

'I have to take a letter to the headquarters of the Russian Army,' said Windischgrätz, slowly and seriously.

'All right, that can be done,' answered Tabakov. 'We'll take you in a moment. But one good turn deserves another. We should like to hold a meeting and invite all your soldiers to it.'

'A meeting? Our soldiers?' And the Austrian officer looked up, with his gleaming black eyes, like olives, at Tabakov standing before him. 'I don't understand. What do you want with our soldiers? I can come, and some other officers, but why do you want our soldiers?'

'No, it's your soldiers we want, not you,' said Tabakov roughly, losing patience.

Windischgrätz looked round suspiciously at the soldiers who encircled him closely, cracking sunflower seeds in a carefree way and smoking his cigarettes. Behind his back the bearded Shapilkin, making funny faces, was silently fingering, over his head, the vents of a big, double-row accordion.

'But what would be discussed at this meeting?' Windischgrätz asked anxiously, after a short pause.

'Questions of war and peace, of brotherhood between peoples, and of revolution. What are you frightened of?' asked Tabakov challengingly, as he felt anger boiling up inside him against this Austrian officer, red-faced and pompous as a turkey.

'Oh no, not at all, I'm not frightened,' replied Windischgrätz, with affected fervour. 'Gentlemen! We are very much in favour of peace. Especially with you Russians: only, for God's sake, in the name of all that's holy, don't meddle in our internal affairs. We know what we want . . . we are a free people!'

At these words there was a deafening roar of laughter.

'Gentlemen, don't you trust me?' asked Windischgrätz, with an affected quaver in his voice.

'I must admit that that is the case,' replied Shapilkin, candidly, and started playing the *Kamarinskaya* on his accordion.

The soldiers were guffawing. Suddenly Windischgrätz realised that he had become a laughing-stock for them. Quickly, he got to his feet, shook down his long-skirted greatcoat and asked to be taken to the headquarters of the Russian Army.

The soldiers conscientiously blindfolded him with a white bandage and, taking him by the arm, led him down the hillock. Out of the corner of his eye he saw grass beneath his feet, and then, after he crossed a shallow ditch, a grey, dusty road, marked by two deep wheel-ruts. The hot sun beat down mercilessly on his back and head.

When they neared regimental headquarters his sweat-soaked bandage was removed and he was put into a roomy, clean and bright ambulance. All wet with perspiration and fatigue, Windischgrätz settled himself with relief on a bunk which was covered with a soft, grey blanket.

For a long time the engine would not start: it snorted, spluttered and at last began working hastily, with misfires, like a sick heart. The ambulance started off with a jerk and, quivering slightly, moved with a rustling sound along the firm surface of the causeway.

The windows of the ambulance had been covered with blue paint. However hard Windischgrätz tried to find some scratch in it, the paint had been applied so thickly, so impenetrably, that nothing could be seen through it. During the whole tedious journey he had to be content with the monotonous walls of the ambulance, like those of a hospital, and the well-painted windows.

Late that evening the ambulance, bumping up and down, rattled over the uneven cobblestones of a small provincial town, and then suddenly stopped. The rear door of the ambulance was opened and a young officer with silver epaulettes and aiguillettes courteously gestured Windischgrätz to alight.

With the agility of a cavalryman and a sportsman, Windischgrätz jumped out on to the cobbled roadway and, escorted by the aide-de-camp, entered a two-storeyed brick building.

IV

Windischgrätz was ushered into the office of General Nekrasov. On the wall hung a green ten-versts-to-the-inch map, with little blue and red flags stuck all over it. From behind the desk, on which papers lay in disorder, rose a strongly-built, young-looking man with a high, steep forehead, a beaky nose and long, curly sideburns. His black hair, streaked with grey, was smoothly parted at the side. Thick, neatly trimmed moustaches were twisted up into sharp points. His brown eyes, with a golden tint in them, had a vigorous, masterful gaze. The left side of his broad chest was completely covered with medals.

The abundance of gold and the blinding gleam recalled some tawdry inconostasis.* Near his heart, on the black-and-yellow ribbon of St George, hung a white enamel cross. At his neck was the Order of St Vladimir, with its crossed swords, slim as rapiers. On his broad epaulettes, with the crown and the monogram, strange zigzags were coiled, as on the back of a viper.

'Captain Ludwig Windischgrätz,' said the Austrian, introducing himself, and with dignity he offered the General his narrow, lean hand, like a chicken's foot. Nekrasov bowed, and then, hastily, as though he had just been scalded, put his right hand behind his back.

'Excuse me, but I cannot give you my hand. You are an enemy of Holy Russia,' said Nekrasov, in the purest French, as he squared his shoulders and threw back his pomaded head, which looked like that of a dog which had just had a bath.

With an imperious, authoritative gesture he invited Windischgrätz to take a seat beside the massive, oak-veneered desk, on which lay one sheet of green blotting-paper fastened with drawing pins. The desk, which was covered with papers, files and opened telegrams, in no sort of order, was decorated with a writing-set that bore a sphinx's head on every item.

Pursing his thin, dry lips, Windischgrätz lowered himself, with an aggrieved air, into the unsteady bentwood chair, which creaked and rocked unexpectedly beneath his weight. He shifted warily on the edge of the chair.

'Circumstances are difficult,' said General Nekrasov gloomily, sitting down in his armchair with the high Gothic back. 'They recognise neither discipline nor God. Do you know what matters have come to? We are in the power of Soviets of Workers' and Soldiers' Deputies.'

Into the room, walking briskly, came a young soldier with a small fair moustache and wearing a red arm-band.

'Where are the latest reports?' he asked Nekrasov quickly,

---

* In Orthodox churches the altar is screened from the nave by a partition covered with holy pictures, often gilded — the 'iconostasis'.

almost without taking breath, and sat down in the empty chair on the other side of the desk from Windischgrätz.

'Here they are,' Nekrasov answered in a curt tone, and handed his visitor a yellow folder.

'There's a meeting of the committee today,' said the young soldier, putting the folder under his arm, and he got up and left.

'There, you see,' observed Nekrasov, who had gone pale, curling his lip and absently turning the key in a drawer of his desk. 'That's what they're like, the members of the soldiers' committee. Come in without knocking, sit down without being asked. No discipline and not the slightest respect for their commanders.'

Windischgrätz, raising high his bristling reddish eyebrows and opening wide his prominent, glassy eyes, listened with great curiosity to Nekrasov's words. He was amazed that an enemy who had refused to shake hands with him should give expression with such frankness to the feelings that were seething within him. However, Nekrasov, having started on this sore subject, could not restrain himself and, encouraged by Windischgrätz's sympathetic air, went on pouring out, with ever greater bitterness, all the pain that two months of revolution had accumulated in his heart.

'Quite so, quite so,' agreed Windischgrätz, and kept nodding his head like the porcelain Chinese figure in the window of a tea-shop.

'I have the honour to bring you a peace-proposal,' he said in a solemn tone, handing Nekrasov a broad white packet sealed with five red seals.

'Good, I'll pass it on to the high command,' was the general's cold reply. Suddenly there was a knock at the door.

'*Prego*,' said Nekrasov, loudly and resonantly. Some time before the war he had been military attaché at Russia's embassy in Rome, and remembered a few words of Italian, which kept turning up in his speech, sometimes appropriately and sometimes not.

Into the room came, walking quickly, lightly and silently, the

General's chief of staff Tarasov. His smoothly shaven head was as round as a billiard ball and a slight hare-lip gave him, despite his forty years, a naïvely childish expression.

Treading noiselessly on the carpet with his soft goatskin boots, he approached the desk and handed Nekrasov a still-damp telegraph form, smelling of glue, with narrow strips of paper stuck on it, bearing printed words.

Nekrasov placed his gold-framed spectacles on his large, hooked nose and bent to read the telegram. Tarasov stood silently before him, his hands unnaturally in line with the seams of his trousers, like a rank-and-file soldier obeying the command 'Attention!' He wanted to show the foreign, enemy officer that there was still discipline in the Russian Army.

With a fixed stare Windischgrätz measured him from head to foot and then, pursing his thin, bloodless lips contemptuously, took his silver cigarette-case out of his pocket, casually bowed the upper half of his body in the General's direction and turned between his fingers and lit a thick, slightly flattened cigarette.

After reading the telegram, Nekrasov initialled it boldly in blue pencil and, after returning it to the chief of staff, took off his spectacles and, his face flushed, leant back in his chair. Silently, like a ghost, Tarasov withdrew.

'Your conduct is unworthy of a soldier,' said Nekrasov, his anger flaring up. 'You want to begin peace negotiations, but at the same time you subvert my troops. This is uncivilised behaviour. I don't wish to have any dealings with you. I warn you that any officer or soldier caught with proclamations on him will be held as a prisoner. You, since you crossed the line of the front under a white flag, I shall allow to return.'

Deathly pale, Windisgrätz jumped up, bowed, and, without saying a word, left the room. The soldier who was waiting outside the door led him down a long, brightly-lit corridor to the office of the counter-intelligence section, a small room with a low ceiling. Ignoring his angry protests, they stripped Windischgrätz and searched him, taking from his pockets and placing on the desk his red morocco wallet, his gold watch, his silver cigarette-case and his linen handkerchiefs with the princely crown and large monogram, embroidered on lace-frames with satin-stitch and an oblique seam. Windischgrätz became very excited and went white and red by turns. He was afraid that they would plant some proclamations under the silk lining of his spiked helmet, so as to have an excuse to arrest him. However, this did not happen.

That night Windischgrätz was returned to the front, in an ambulance with whitewashed windows, and at dawn, blindfolded, he was sent back to the Austrian trenches. When they removed his bandage he screwed up his eyes, blinded by the bright, oblique rays of the still unwarming morning sun. Looking around him, he saw that, despite the early hour, fraternisation was in full swing. Suddenly, two Russian soldiers led past him an Austrian soldier they had arrested because he was carrying a small packet of proclamations, printed on thin cigarette-paper by Windischgrätz's own order, calling on Russian soldiers to give themselves up.

Windischgrätz was astonished to see that, despite this arrest, other Austrian soldiers continued, as though nothing had happened, calmly and coolly to smoke and chat with the Russians.

V

Prince Windischgrätz was pleased with the results of his risky trip into the Russian rear. The information which the Russian soldiers had refused to give him, he had obtained from General Nekrasov. From what Nekrasov had said, Windischgrätz was able, just as when from a shard one reconstructs a whole vase, to form a clear picture of the disintegration of the Russian army.

Back in the Austrian trenches, Windischgrätz was at once surrounded by officer acquaintances. After rapidly telling them of the impressions he had formed, he wanted to push on, using the duty motor-cycle, so as to hand in his report at headquarters. Then, suddenly, they heard the roar of a distant gun, and from the open, green clearing where for two days and nights Russian and Austrian soldiers had been peacefully fraternising rose a tall, grey-black column of earth and smoke.

In the blue sky a curly white cloud burst and slowly broke up. Shrapnel was scattered on the heads of the fraternising soldiers. Fragments embedded themselves violently in the ground, uprooting the grass. Russians and Austrians rushed helter-skelter back to their respective trenches.

'Have we got to climb on to that damned *sopka* again?' exclaimed Shapilkin, angrily. 'When you're lying there under the enemy's machine-gun fire, you curse everything.'

'What's happened?' the soldiers asked as they ran. In the confusion, two Austrians ran into a Russian trench.

It soon became clear that it was a Russian battery that had opened fire. The battery commander, a colonel with long mous-taches, angry about the fraternisation that was going on, had ordered that the gathering in the 'valley of death' be dispersed.

The Russian cannonade evoked fury in the Austrian camp. The Austrians were indignant that the Russians, after luring them into fraternisation, were now firing on them.

Zhivets was still in one of the Austrian trenches.

'Ah, so this is the way you behave! It's all a trick!' shouted Windischgrätz in unrestrained anger, and his glassy, prom-inent eyes protruded even further than usual.

Not knowing what to do, Zhivets, like a trapped hare, backed against the cold, damp wall of the trench.

Windischgrätz summoned a detachment of soldiers who, at his command, aimed their rifles at Zhivets. Vigorously drawing his sharp sword from its long black scabbard, Windischgrätz brandished it in the air. An irregular volley rang out. Stepan clutched his chest, which had been pierced by a sharp, burning pain. His legs gave way and, like a felled tree, he toppled backward, convulsively scrabbling with his fingers at the damp earth. He wanted to cry out, to howl with pain, but he could only give a feeble groan. With extraordinary clarity he sud-denly saw his mother, her red head-scarf tied high, her large sorrowful eyes. He felt an excruciating pity for her, and cried out.

'Finish him off!' ordered Windischgrätz, addressing a short Austrian soldier with a thick black stubble on his cheeks.

A revolver shot rang out. This time the bullet reached the heart. For one moment Stepan felt an unbearable, absolutely inuman pain, then everything became confused, going round and round, and he lost consciousness. Instead of a face that was red as though scalded there was now a pale waxen mask.

The battery-commander who gave the order to fire on the men who were fraternising was tossed by the soldiers on their bayonets.

Next morning, the Austrian soldiers were told the reason for the fatal gunfire. Fraternisation was resumed with fresh enthusiasm. When, in the autumn of the following year, a revolution took place in Austria-Hungary, Wurstmacher and others of the Austrians who had fraternised, remembering the slogan of the great Lenin about turning the imperialist war into a civil war, were in the foremost columns of the crowd that stormed the Palace of Schönbrunn and overthrew the centuries-old monarchy of the Habsburgs.*

---

* There was, in fact, no storming of the Palace of Schönbrunn. The Emperor gave in without a fight. One of the leaders of the Austrian Republic created in 1918 wrote about the revolution in Vienna: 'The object had been accomplished in the course of six weeks without street fighting or civil war, without using force or shedding blood. To be sure, like every other revolution, this one was a work of force. But the force which rendered the revolution possible was not expended in the streets of Vienna. On the battlefields, in the Balkans and in Venetia, it smashed the obsolete mechanism which stood in the way of the revolution. Consequently, we were able to make the revolution at home without force.' (Otto Bauer, *The Austrian Revolution* [1925], p.65.)

Raskolnikov's
Open Letter to Stalin

This document, dated August 17, 1939, was first published in the Paris émigré newspaper *Novaya Rossiya* of October 1, 1939. According to Roy Medvedev, *Let History Judge,* (p.257), in 1964 the author's widow, a resident of France, brought the original of the letter to Moscow. It circulated widely through *samizdat* channels in the mid-1960s. The translator is indebted to the Current Affairs Research Section of the BBC's External Services for a copy of the *samizdat* edition.

> *I shall tell that truth about you*
> *Which is worse than any lie.**

Stalin, you have proclaimed that I am an 'outlaw'. By so doing you have given me the same rights — or, more precisely, the same lack of rights — as all Soviet citizens, who under your rule live as outlaws.

For my part, I answer you with complete reciprocity: I return to you the entrance ticket into the 'realm of socialism' you have built, and break with your regime. Your 'socialism', which, now it has triumphed, can find room for those who built it only behind prison bars, is just as remote from real socialism as the tyranny of your personal dictatorship is without anything in common with the dictatorship of the proletariat.

---

* From Griboyedov's play *Woe from Wit*, Act III, Scene 9.

It is of no help to you if the respected *Narodnaya Volya* revolutionary N.A. Morozov, decorated with an Order, affirms that it was for this 'socialism' that he spent twenty years of his life under the vaults of Schlüsselburg fortress.*

The elemental growth of discontent among the workers, peasants and intelligentsia called imperatively for a sharp political manoeuvre comparable to Lenin's turn towards the New Economic Policy in 1921. Under the pressure of the Soviet people you 'granted' a democratic constitution. It was received by the whole country with sincere enthusiasm.

An honest implementation of the democratic principles of the constitution of 1936, which embodied the hopes and aspirations of the entire people, would have meant a new stage in the extension of Soviet democracy.

But, in your mind, every political manoeuvre is synonymous with cheating and deception. You have cultivated a kind of politics without morality, authority without honesty, socialism without love for mankind.

What have you done with the constitution, Stalin?

Fearing free elections as a 'leap into the unknown' that would threaten your personal power, you have trampled on the constitution as though it were just a bit of paper, you have transformed elections in a miserable farce of voting for a single candidate, and you have filled the sessions of the Supreme Soviet with hymns and ovations in honour of yourself. In the intervals between sessions you quietly annihilate the 'ingratiated' deputies, laughing at their immunity and reminding everyone that the master of the Soviet land is not the Supreme Soviet but yourself.

You have done everything you could to discredit Soviet democracy, just as you have discredited socialism. Instead of

---

* N.A. Morozov (1854-1946), a leader of the Narodnaya Volya terrorist organisation, spent the years 1882-1905 as a prisoner in Schlüsselburg fortress. After the October Revolution, he was given the Order of Lenin and the Order of the Red Banner, and made an Honorary Academician. Raskolnikov refers to the statements in praise of Stalin made by Morozov in his old age.

following the line of the turn indicated by the constitution, you are suppressing the growing discontent by force and terror. Having gradually replaced the dictatorship of the proletariat by the regime of your personal dictatorship, you have opened a new stage which will enter into the history of our revolution as 'the epoch of terror'.

Nobody in the Soviet Union feels safe. Nobody, when he goes to bed, knows if he will escape arrest during the night. There is no mercy for anyone. The righteous and the guilty, the hero of October and the enemy of the revolution, the old Bolshevik and the non-party man, the collective-farm peasant and the ambassador, the People's Commissar and the worker, the intellectual and the Marshal of the Soviet Union — all are equally subject to the blows of your scourge, all are whirled in your bloody devil's roundabout.

Just as, when a volcano erupts, huge boulders crash thunderously into the mouth of the crater, so whole strata of Soviet society are being broken off and are falling into the abyss.

You began with bloody measures against former Trotskyists, Zinovievists and Bukharinists, then you proceeded to exterminate the old Bolsheviks, then you destroyed the Party and non-party cadres that grew up during the civil war and bore on their shoulders the task of carrying through the first Five-Year Plans, and then you organised a massacre of the Young Communist League.

You hide behind the slogan of struggle against 'Trotskyist-Bukharinist spies'. But it is not since yesterday that you have held power. Nobody could have 'insinuated' himself into a post of responsibility without your permission.

Who put the so-called 'enemies of the people' into the most responsible positions in the state, the Party, the army and the diplomatic service? Joseph Stalin.

Who planted the so-called 'wreckers' in all the crevices of the Party and Soviet apparatus? Joseph Stalin.

Read the old minutes of the Politbureau: they are filled with appointments and postings of none but 'Trotskyist-Bukharinist

spies', 'wreckers' and 'diversionists' — and beneath them
flaunts the signature: J. Stalin.

You make yourself out to have been a trusting simpleton
whom some carnival monsters wearing masks have led by the
nose for years on end.

'Seek out and prepare the scapegoats,' you whisper to your
henchmen, and those who are caught and doomed to be sac-
rificed you load with the sins you have yourself committed.

You have fettered the country by means of fearful terror, so
that even a brave man does not dare to cast the truth in your
face.

The waves of self-criticism 'without respect of persons' die
away respectfully at the footstool of your throne.

You are infallible, like the Pope! You never make a mistake!

But the Soviet people know very well that you are responsible
for everything, you, the smith who is forging 'universal happiness'!

With the aid of dirty forgeries you staged trials in which the
preposterousness of the accusations surpasses the mediaeval
witch-trials you learnt about from your seminary textbooks.

You know that Pyatakov did not fly to Oslo, that Maxim
Gorky died a natural death, and that Trotsky did not derail any
trains. Aware that that is all lies, you spur on your minions:
'Slander away: from slander something will always stick.'

As you know, I was never a Trotskyist. On the contrary, I
waged an ideological struggle against all the oppositions, both
in the press and in broad meetings. Today as well I do not agree
with Trotsky's political position, with his programme and tactics. While differing with Trotsky on points of principle, I
regard him as an honest revolutionary. I do not believe and
never shall believe in his 'compact' with Hitler and Hess.

You are a cook who prepares highly-spiced dishes that are
indigestible for normal people.

At Lenin's tomb you swore a solemn oath to fulfil his testament and to preserve the unity of the Party like the apple of
your eye. Perjurer, you have violated Lenin's testament. You

have calumniated, dishonoured and shot those who for many years were Lenin's companions in arms: Kamenev, Zinoviev, Bukharin, Rykov and others, of whose innocence you were well aware. Before they died you forced them to confess to crimes they never committed and to smear themselves with filth from head to foot.

And where are the heroes of the October Revolution? Where is Bubnov? Where is Krylenko? Where is Antonov-Ovseyenko? Where is Dybenko? You arrested them, Stalin.*

You corrupted and befouled the souls of your collaborators. You compelled your followers to wade, in anguish and disgust, through pools of blood shed by their comrades and friends of yesterday.

In the lying history of the Party written under your direction you robbed the dead, those whom you had murdered and defamed, and took for yourself all their achievements and services.

You destroyed Lenin's Party, and on its bones you erected a new 'Party of Lenin and Stalin' which forms a convenient screen for your autocracy. You created it not on the basis of a common programme and tactics, as any party is built, but on the unprincipled basis of love and devotion towards your person. Members of the new Party are not obliged to know its programme, but instead they are obliged to share that love for Stalin which is warmed up every day by the press.   You are a renegade who has broken with his past and betrayed Lenin's cause!

You solemnly proclaimed the slogan of advancement of new cadres. But how many of these young promotees are already rotting in your dungeons? How many of them have you shot, Stalin? With sadistic cruelty you exterminate cadres that are useful and necessary to the country, because they seem to you dangerous from the standpoint of your personal dictatorship.

---

* In another version of the 'Open Letter', the following words appear at this point: 'Where is the Old Guard? You shot them, Stalin.' — *B.P.*

On the eve of war you disrupt the Red Army, the love and pride of our country, the bulwark of its might. You have beheaded the Red Army and the Red Navy. You have killed the most talented commanders, those who were educated through experience in the world war and the civil war, headed by the brilliant Marshal Tukhachevsky. You exterminated the heroes of the civil war, who had reorganised the Red Army in accordance with the most up-to-date military technique, and made it invincible.

At the moment of the greatest danger of war you are continuing to exterminate the leaders of the Army, and the middle-ranking and junior commanders as well.

Where is Marshal Blücher? Where is Marshal Yegorov? You arrested them, Stalin.

To calm anxious minds you deceive the country by saying that the Red Army, weakened by these arrests and executions, has become even stronger than before.

Although you know that the law of military science demands one-man command in the army, from the commander-in-chief down to the platoon commander, you have revived the institution of political commissars, which arose in the early days of the Red Army and the Red Navy, when we did not yet have commanders of our own, and needed to exercise political supervision over military specialists drawn from the old army. Out of distrust of the Red commanders you are introducing divided authority into the Army and undermining military discipline.

Under pressure from the Russian people you are hypocritically reviving the cult of the heroes of Russia's history — Alexander Nevsky and Dmitri Donskoi, Suvorov and Kutuzov — in the hope that in the coming war they will help you more than the Marshals and Generals you have executed.

Exploiting your distrust of everybody, genuine agents of the Gestapo and the Japanese intelligence service fish successfully in the troubled waters you have stirred up, palming off on you quantities of false documents to blacken the best, most talented and honest people. In the poisoned atmosphere of suspicion, mutual distrust, universal spying and omnipotence of the People's Commissariat of Internal Affairs to which you have handed over for rending the Red Army and the whole country, any intercepted 'document' is accepted — or a pretence is made that it is accepted — as indisputable proof. By slipping to Yezhov's agents forged documents which compromise honest members of the mission, the 'internal service of the ROVs', in the person of Captain Voss, has managed to destroy our Embassy in Bulgaria, from the driver M.I. Kazakov to the military attaché Colonel V.T. Sukhorukov.*

You are annihilating the most important conquests of October one after the other. On the pretext of combating 'fluctuation in labour-power' you have abolished freedom of labour, enslaved the Soviet workers and bound them to the factories. You have ruined the country's economic organism, disorganised industry and transport, undermined the authority of the manager, the engineer and the foreman, accompanying the ceaseless leap-frog of dismissals and appointments with arrests and hounding of engineers, managers and workers whom you call 'hidden wreckers, not yet exposed'.

After making normal work impossible, you have, on the pretext of combating 'absenteeism' and 'lateness' on the part of the workers, forced them to work under the whips and scorpions of harsh and anti-proletarian decrees.

Your inhuman repressions are making life unbearable for the Soviet working people, who for the slightest offence are dismissed from their jobs, with a record that damns them, and evicted from their homes.

The working class bore with selfless heroism the burdens of

---

* 'ROVS' are the initials of the Russian name of the 'Russian General Military Union', the organisation of the ex-soldiers of the White Armies living as émigrés in Europe. In 1927 Captain K.A. Voss, chief of staff of the head of ROVS in Bulgaria, formed an 'internal service' for the alleged purpose of carrying on secret intelligence work against the USSR. In 1938, however, after a number of incidents had aroused suspicion that Voss and his associates were actually double agents, the ROVS leadership dissolved this 'internal service'. Voss is said to have worked for the Gestapo in Russia during the German invasion.

intense labour, undernourishment, famine, meagre wages, cramped living-space and lack of necessities. They believed that you would lead them to socialism, but you have betrayed their trust. They hoped that, with the victory of socialism in our country, when the dream of humanity's brilliant minds about a great brotherhood of mankind had been accomplished, all would live in happiness and ease.

You have taken away even that hope: you have proclaimed that socialism has already been fully built. And the workers, bewildered, ask each other, in whispers: 'If this is socialism, then what, comrades, did we fight for?'

Distorting Lenin's theory of the withering away of the state, as you have distorted the entire theory of Marxism-Leninism, you promise, through the mouths of your illiterate, primitive 'theoreticians', who have occupied the places left vacant by Bukharin, Kamenev and Lunacharsky, that the power of the GPU will be maintained even under communism.*

You have deprived the collective farm peasants of every incentive to work. On the pretext of combating 'the squandering of collective-farm land' you have abolished their individual plots of land, so as to force them to work in the collective-farm fields.†

As the organiser of famine you have done everything possible, by the brutality and cruelty of the unscrupulous methods that are typical of your tactics, to discredit Lenin's idea of collectivisation in the eyes of the peasantry.

While hypocritically calling the intelligentsia 'the salt of the earth' you have deprived the work of the writer, the scholar and the artist of even the minimum of inner freedom. You have forced art into a straitjacket in which it suffocates, withers and

---

* In another version of the letter, the following words appear at this point: 'There is nothing to stop you announcing tomorrow that communism has been established. Crude vulgariser that you are, you have done everything possible to discredit Lenin's theory of the building of socialism in one country.' — *B.P.*

† In another version of the letter, the following words appear at this point: 'In your mockery of the collective-farm peasants, you have gone so far as to impose a meat-tax levied not per head of cattle but per hectare of land.' — *B.P.*

dies. The frenzy of the censorship, inspired by fear of you, and the understandable servility of editors who answer for everything with their heads, have led to sclerosis and paralysis in Soviet literature. A writer cannot get into print, a playwright cannot put his plays on the stage, a critic cannot express his personal opinion, unless he has received the official seal of approval.

You stifle Soviet art by demanding that it display courtier-like bootlicking, but it prefers to stay silent, so as not to sing Hosannas in praise of you. You are introducing a pseudo-art which hymns with boring monotony that famous 'genius' of yours which sets one's teeth on edge.

Untalented scribblers glorify you as a demi-god, 'born of the Sun and the Moon', and you, like an Oriental despot, delight in the incense of their crude flattery.

You pitilessly crush Russian writers who, though talented, are not to your liking. Where is Boris Pilnyak? Where is Sergei Tretyakov? Where is Alexander Arosev? Where is Mikhail Koltsov? Where is Tarasov-Rodionov? Where is Galina Serebryakova, whose crime was to be Sokolnikov's wife? You arrested them, Stalin!

Following Hitler's example, you have revived the mediaeval burning of books. I have seen with my own eyes the long lists, circulated to Soviet libraries, of books that are to be subjected to immediate and unconditional destruction. When I was ambassador in Bulgaria in 1937 I found in the list of forbidden literature to be burnt which was sent to me my own work of historical reminiscences, *Kronstadt and Petrograd in 1917*. Against the names of many authors was written: 'All books, pamphlets and portraits to be destroyed.'

---

* Alexander Arosev (mentioned above, p.356, as Muralov's deputy in Moscow), gave particular offence to Stalin as a writer by his book, *Korni* (The Roots), published in 1933. The novel depicts the workings of the Bolshevik underground organisation in Tsarist times. 'The character of Vano, a silent, sullen man, eternally smoking a pipe, was apparently intended to represent Stalin. Vano's pride suffers because he is merely one of many instead of the top man, and this injured pride breeds distrust, bitterness and contempt for others.' (V. Zavashilin, *Early Soviet Writers*, 1958, p.210.)

You have deprived Soviet scholars — especially those working in the humanities — of that minimum of freedom of scientific thought without which the creative work of research becomes impossible. By means of intrigue, troublemaking and persecution, self-assured ignoramuses are preventing scholars and scientists from working in the universities, laboratories and institutes.

Outstanding Russian men of learning, of world-wide fame, like Academicians Ipatiev and Chichibabin,* you have denounced to the whole world as 'non-returners', naively supposing that thereby you defame them, but you only disgrace yourself, by making known to the whole country and to world public opinion the shameful fact that the best scholars and scientists flee from your paradise, leaving to you the 'benefits' you confer: flats, motor-cars and tickets of admission to the dining-room of the Council of People's Commissars.

You are exterminating talented Russian scholars and scientists. Where is Tupolev, the best Soviet aeroplane-designer? You have not spared even him. You arrested Tupolev, Stalin!

No field, no corner is left in which one can tranquilly carry on the work one loves. The theatrical director, remarkable producer and outstanding artist Vsevolod Meyerhold did not engage in politics. But you arrested him too, Stalin!

Although you know that, given our poverty in cadres, every educated and experienced diplomat is particularly precious to us, you have enticed to Moscow and destroyed nearly all the Soviet Union's ambassadors, one after another. You have thoroughly destroyed the entire apparatus of the People's Commissariat of Foreign Affairs. Destroying here, there and everywhere the gold reserve of our country, its young cadres, you have exterminated talented and promising diplomats in the flower of their lives.

At a terrible moment of war-danger, when the spearhead of

* V.N. Ipatiev (1867-1952) and A.E. Chichibabin (1871-1945), both distinguished organic chemists, 'failed to return' from visits abroad in 1930. Ipatiev's autobiography, *The Life of a Chemist* (1946), describes the experiences which led him to 'defect'.

fascism is aimed at the Soviet Union, when the struggle over Danzig and the war in China are merely preparing *places d'armes* for future intervention against the USSR, when the principal object of German and Japanese aggression is our motherland, when the only possible means of preventing war is for the Soviet Union to enter openly into the international bloc of democratic states, concluding as soon as may be a military and political pact with Britain and France, you waver, hesitate, vacillate like a pendulum between the 'axes'.

In all your calculations in politics, both external and internal, you proceed not from love for the motherland, which is alien to you, but from animal fear of losing your personal power. Your unprincipled dictatorship blocks our country's way forward, like a rotten log.

You, 'the Father of the Peoples', betrayed the defeated Spanish revolutionaries, abandoning them to the will of fate and leaving other states to look after them. Magnanimous saving of human lives is not included among your principles. Woe to the conquered! You have no further need of them.

You have callously doomed the Jewish workers, intellectuals and craftsmen fleeing from Fascist barbarism, by shutting against them the doors of our country, which could hospitably offer refuge in its immense spaces to many thousands of immigrants.

Like all Soviet patriots, I got on with my work while closing my eyes to many things. I kept silent for too long. It was hard for me to break my last ties — not with you, your doomed regime, but with the remains of Lenin's old Party, of which I had been a member for nearly thirty years, and which you destroyed in three. It was agonisingly painful to be deprived of my motherland.

More and more, as time goes by, the interests of your personal dictatorship will come into irreconcilable conflict with the interests of the workers, the peasants, the intelligentsia, the interests of the whole country, which you mock, as a tyrant who has risen to personal power.

Your social basis is shrinking day by day. Feverishly seeking support, you lavish hypocritical compliments on the 'non-Party Bolsheviks', you create new privileged groups one after another, you heap favours upon them, you feed them sops, but you cannot guarantee these new 'caliphs for an hour' not only the retention of their privileges but even their right to live.

Your crazy bacchanal cannot last for long. The list of your crimes is endless! Endless is the roll-call of your victims! It is impossible to enumerate them.

Sooner or later, the Soviet people will put you in the dock as a traitor to socialism and the revolution, the chief wrecker, the real enemy of the people, the organiser of famine and of judicial forgeries.

F. Raskolnikov
August 17, 1939

Glossary of names

AVILOV, N.P. (Glebov), 1887-1942. Died in prison.

AVILOV, S.S., 1877-1939. Died in prison.

AZIN, V.M., 1895-1920. A Red Army commander captured and executed by the Whites.

BONCH-BRUYEVICH, V.D., 1873-1955.

BUBNOV, A.S., 1883-1940. Died in prison.

DYBENKO, P.E., 1889-1938. A Baltic Fleet sailor who figures in Raskolnikov's *Kronstadt and Petrograd in 1917*. Executed.

GAVEN, Yu.P. (Dauman), 1884-1936. A Party member since 1902, chairman of the Party Committee at Sebastopol. He may have died in prison.

GLYASSER, M.I., 1890-1951.

KERRAN, F.L. (originally Kehrhahn), born 1883, a member of the Hackney branch of the BSP, was interned on the grounds of his German origin, but escaped. When caught, he was imprisoned. He became a foundation member of the Communist Party of Great Britain, but left the Party in 1924.

KIKVIDZE, V.I., 1895-1919. See Trotsky, *How the Revolution Armed*, Volume Two, pp.28 and 249.

KNIPOVICH, B.N., 1890-1924. In the early 1920s published works dealing with regional planning for agriculture in Russia.

KNIPOVICH, L.M., 1856-1920, had been a Social-Democrat since the 1890s.

KOZHANOV, I.K., 1897-1938. Died in prison.

KUKEL, V.A. (Krayevsky), 1885-1940, later chief of staff of the Volga-Caspian flotilla. He may have died in prison.

LAVROV, P.L., 1823-1900. Influential Narodnik writer.

LOMOV, A. (G.I. Oppokov), 1888-1938. A party member from the beginning; executed.

MEKHONOSHIN, K.A., 1889-1938. Was Deputy People's Commissar for Military Affairs in 1918. Died in prison.

MIKHAILOVSKY, N.K., 1842-1904. Influential Narodnik writer.

MINOR, O.S., 1861-1932(?). An S-R activist, he had returned from exile in Siberia in 1909-1917 to become chairman of Moscow City Council.

NEMITZ, A.V., 1879-1967. Commander of Soviet Naval Forces, February 1920-December 1921.

NEVSKY, V.I., 1876-1937. Died in prison.

OSTROVSKAYA, N.I., Party member since 1911; had been a member of the Military Revolutionary Committee at Sebastopol.

PAYKES, A.K., 1873-1958. Until the October Revolution was a Menshevik, but went over to the Bolsheviks in 1918.

PETROV, G.K., 1892-1918.

PHILLIPS OPPENHEIM, E., 1866-1946, was a popular writer of romances of intrigue, often set in Monte Carlo.

RAKHIYA, I.A., 1887-1920.

RUBIN, I.I., 1883-1918. Chairman of the Presidium of the Black-Sea-Kuban Republic, was murdered by I.L. Sorokin, commander of the 11th Red Army, when he revolted against the Soviet Government in October 1918.

SHLYAPNIKOV, A.G., 1885-1943. Died in prison.

SHORIN, V.I., 1870-1938. Died in prison.

SHVETSOV, S.P., 1858-1930. Had been exiled to Siberia in 1879. He was a founder-member of the Socialist-Revolutionary Party.

SIEVERS, R.F., 1892-1918.

SKVORTSOV-STEPANOV, I.I., 1870-1928. A Party member from the beginning.

SMIDOVICH, P.G., 1874-1935.

VAKHRAMEYEV, I.I., 1885-1965. He reached Novorossiisk on June 2.

YAKOVLEVA, V.N., 1884-1944. Died in prison.

ZHELEZNYAKOV, A.G., 1895-1919. An Anarchist sailor from Kronstadt.

Index